CONFESSIONS
OF A
CONFORMIST

MORRIS
FREEDMAN

CONFESSIONS OF A CONFORMIST

W · W · NORTON & COMPANY · INC · *New York*

FIRST EDITION

Library of Congress Catalog Card No. 61-5343

PRINTED IN THE UNITED STATES OF AMERICA
FOR THE PUBLISHERS BY THE VAIL-BALLOU PRESS

1 2 3 4 5 6 7 8 9

To Charlotte

CONTENTS

CONFESSIONS
OF A
CONFORMIST

ONE

THE DANGERS OF NONCONFORMISM

NOT LONG ago I heard one of this country's professional intellectuals, Robert Maynard Hutchins—a former university president, a present foundation president—address a university gathering of several hundred persons. Mr. Hutchins attacked the blight of conformism in the United States; he deplored the fact that men in gray flannel suits had become "interchangeable"; he lamented the loss of true individualism. I agreed with much of what he said, and what I did not agree with is not quite my point at present. What struck me while listening to his urbane talk was his own "interchangeable" appearance: neat, three-button blue suit, plain tie, precisely coiffured graying hair, erect carriage: the very model of a model executive, not only interchangeable with dozens of men in similar positions and in "gentlemen of distinction" ads, but ready to be played in the movies by a dozen or so actors—Walter Pidgeon, Cary Grant, Gregory Peck, Ray Milland. It struck me as somewhat odd, too, that several hundred persons should applaud in unison a speech urging nonconformity, and that during the question period one of the questions that did not "conform" with the speaker's views should be greeted with derision by both speaker and audience.

Of course one man's conformism may be another man's heresy. But what seems to have taken place in American intellectual life in recent years is the rising of just about any nonconformity to the status of respectable orthodoxy. It is even more strange that it has become as risky to attack these nonconformist orthodoxies as it ever was to attack a conformist one. These days the best protection is to become a nonconformist. In Mary McCarthy's novel about academic life, *The Groves of Academe*, the central character withstands an attempt by the liberal college administration to fire him for incompetence by falsely claiming to be a Communist. The nonconformist orthodoxy in that environment clearly required being more than fair with Communists, and the professor changed color accordingly. Indeed, it is probably more comfortable today on many campuses to be politically radical than politically conservative. One sure way of getting a job in an advertising agency, I have been told, is to insist that you are an angry young rebel.

The terms "conformity" and "nonconformity" have been so abused in recent years, it may be necessary to define them early for the purposes of this book. "Conformist" is a term of contempt and insult these days; anyone professing "conformism" on any issue is expected promptly to apologize, or at least to put his position defiantly or defensively if he is to retain a modicum of respect. The conformist is simply one who takes a conventional, usual, generally "majority" position.

The nonconformist, who wears his label with a flamboyant proudness, insists that only departure from convention, the championing of the unusual, the automatic rejection of the majority, will guarantee enlightenment or progress. So aggressively has the professional working nonconformist established his values that anyone, conformist or individualist, who wants to demur on a particular dogma runs the risk of social ostracism. As things go these days, it is the conformist who is made to feel inferior and to knuckle under to the nonconformist.

The question of conformity, of course, exercises only those certain portions of the American population that loosely may be called the "intellectual" circles. College communities undoubtedly form the largest of these, although the publishing, advertising, and entertainment circles are not insubstantial. The issue of conformity scarcely exists for others, the majority, who conform automatically and happily, without giving the question a second thought. Nonconformists have this majority in mind when they attack conformity. They condemn this majority for deriding individual differences, for responding in herd-fashion to the blandishments of advertising and public-relations experts, for being responsible for mass taste and mass opinion. No doubt the nonconformists are right in all of these charges. Yet it may easily be shown that the self-elected nonconformists are culpable on every count on which they attack conformists.

I am sure I am not alone in observing that nonconformists, instead of responding to the values of tabloid newspaper, subway car or television advertisements, respond to a no less specific and no less rigid set, particularly those in the advertisements of the *New York Times*, the *New Yorker*, the *Saturday Review* and the like, or of the commercials of FM stations that broadcast classical music all day. Although the nonconformist may refuse, with a shudder, to engage in the barbaric practice of drinking instant coffee, he will no less eagerly sip espresso. He will avoid a "morning coffee" with lunch or dinner, just as the advertisements tell him to. If you can construct a stereotype of the man in the street, you can build an equally plausible one of the man out of the street. Of course, as I say, this proposition is not new, as was definitively demonstrated by Russell Lynes's wickedly clever classifications some while ago in *Life* of the habits of lowbrow, middlebrow and highbrow (classifications which themselves no doubt helped establish new laws of how not to conform).

Were all this merely a matter of an amusing sociological pastime—observing and arranging the eating, drinking, dressing, entertainment, furniture-buying, political and general ideological habits of low-, middle-, and highbrows, or of conformists and nonconformists—there would not be much point in bringing up the matter again after Lynes, Riesman, and others have settled it so exhaustively. Actually, however, much more is involved. It seems to me that the orthodoxy of the nonconformists is especially dangerous since it claims to be the result of free investigation and free thought, the product of the uncontrolled, individual mind. An orthodoxy clearly related to some conformist dogma we can so much more easily accept or reject on its own basis.

Let me cite the subject of education from among a number I might have chosen. The country is engaged in a major debate on the problem: the debate is quite limited, on one side to the professional educators, referred to as "educationists" by the opposition; and on the other, to what might be called the humanists, many of whom would also proudly claim the title of nonconformists (for they refuse to accept the majority attitude toward education).

Now, I like to think of myself as among the humanists; and I am certainly appalled by the more extreme notions of educators who believe in teaching the "whole child" (presumably to the suppression of any talented part of him), who believe in teaching "life adjustment" rather than subject matter, who believe in "social promotion," et cetera, et cetera, ad nauseam. I hold that persons who believe such things without qualification should be opposed vigorously; I believe that they should not have final or exclusive say about the schooling of American children, as they now do in many places. But having said this, I must also say that I do not think that the professional educators are to a man villains or idiots—as many critics of them do say or come close to saying.

I probably would not have come to this last conclusion, mild as it may seem, except for the excess and inconsistency of the professional nonconformists on the subject of education. Like nonconformists elsewhere, the nonconformist here prefers to deal with abstractions rather than with reality. One of the many realities of the problem of American education is surely the immense compulsion for universal schooling. Most states have some kind of law compelling attendance in school of every young person up to a certain age regardless of his willingness to learn. I do not say that such laws offer a blanket excuse to educators for their positions, but these laws, the result of great community pressures in the past, are almost always neglected by extremist critics of the schools who insist on an across-the-board raising of standards. Nor have I seen critics of the schools consider the broader pressures in American life that tend to make American education the very special thing that it is.

Consider *Life* magazine's much-publicized first issue in

a series on the "Crisis in Education." It condemns the casual diffuseness of American schools by contrast with the concentrated seriousness of Russian ones. The day of a Russian boy and the day of an American boy of the same age are compared, both in school and after. As one might expect, the American boy is inept at mathematics, which he takes as a joke; he tosses off his homework; he is adept only at rock-'n-roll and swimming. In short, the American boy is typical of many American young people, who, among other things, are interested in finding out about the making of a movie, or looking at scantily dressed young actresses changing costumes, or reading about horse-racing and the latest trend in cars, or going to church to see their minister perform tricks of magic, or looking at the new fashions in clothes and carpets—or reading the latest *Life*, which, in addition to criticizing American education, devoted that same issue to covering all of these edifying and instructive aspects of the broad American scene for its readers. *Life* magazine itself is certainly one of the main forces in making American life what it is; yet the editors, I am sure, would never think of blaming themselves for emphasizing values possibly inimical to seriousness in education. (Perhaps I ought to mention that I do not belong to the nonconformist faction which criticizes *Life;* all in all, if anyone cares, I think the magazine is all right.)

It was not so long ago that a position taken by a Luce publication would have been instinctively opposed by large numbers of nonconformists; but *Life* in recent years has so well caught the importance of being fashionably nonconformist that it is now a leader in establishing accepted nonconformist thought, which, of course, some while ago spilled over from the highbrow crest onto the extensive middlebrow plateaus. On the matter of education, *Life* and other media shaping mass nonconformist ideology have now laid down the party line, making it intellectually suicidal to suggest that possibly the educators have their own peculiar problems to solve before they can reshape their curricula to respond to the present pressures. On most campuses, I venture, a professor in liberal arts would be read out of the ranks if he said a good word about colleges of education, let alone about educational television, which combines two bogeys.

The pressure of nonconformists to force an unmodulated conformity to their present position on education makes it extremely difficult for humanists of good will to conduct that "dialogue" with the educators which the foundation president I spoke of earlier insisted is necessary for understanding and progress. Perhaps it is an exaggeration, even a distortion, to say that nonconformists, like Communists of old, insist on free speech for themselves but not for their opponents; certainly one is tempted to think this when a woman in the audience I mentioned made a remark favorable to the schools and was answered with a quip from the speaker and jeers from the audience.

I have spent this much time on education because the danger of intransigent nonconformism seems to me greatest at this moment in that area; nonconformist opposition may yet do as much damage to American education as the educators themselves have done—although I concede it would probably take nonconformism a long time to establish a record of equal harm. The dangers of nonconformism are to be found wherever opinions, tastes, standards, judgments, and beliefs are operative. Let me catalogue from my own recent experience a number of positions, attitudes, and habits of behavior and thought no nonconformist in good standing can hold these days. These are, of course, subject to rapid change, like fashions in ladies' dress. Also, I should say, it is not essential to reject *all* to remain a respectable nonconformist—only most of them.

It seems impossible, then, for the nonconformist to say a good word about a Republican or a Southern or Texas Democrat or (since Dwight MacDonald's critique in *Commentary*) James Gould Cozzens, or a bad one about Henry James, Adlai Stevenson, Franklin D. Roosevelt, or Freud. It is impossible for a nonconformist to express approval of any television show (except such as *Omnibus*, Ed Murrow, Mort Sahl, Sid Caesar, or Mike Nichols and Elaine May) or of any American movie (except the inexpensive and badly lighted ones, or the solemn westerns, like *High Noon*); to dislike any foreign films (except those imitating American ones); to believe that you can buy ready-made a good hi-fi set; to wear a non-Ivy-league suit or long hair if a man; to prefer American cars, for any reason, to European. It is impossible for a nonconformist to believe that there may be any justice in the official position on Oppenheimer; to defend Western diplomacy on any basis; to invite company to dinner without candles on the table and without chamber music in the background. It is impossible to criticize Arthur Miller or Tennessee Williams as playwrights or otherwise (of course, the shifting popularity of each is constantly causing nonconformist adjustments); to like Tschaikovsky or Irving Berlin, or dislike Leonard Bernstein or Mozart; to express admiration for Marilyn Monroe or any other American movie star; to disparage Alec Guinness; and so on and on.

Since some of the items I list are clearly considered

heinous heresies in some quarters and likely to cost individuals professing them their jobs or at least their reputations, I hasten to add that I know no one guilty of more than one of them; as for myself, at the moment I plead the Fifth Amendment. Nor is this altogether frivolous, for I do know of one college teacher who did not have his contract renewed at least in part for his persistent advocacy of the conformist Southern position on segregation; and I know of one junior executive in advertising who will always remain junior because he occasionally wears a double-breasted, navy-blue Cheviot suit with brown shoes—"like a subway rider reading the *Daily News*," he was described to me by a disapproving colleague (his competence was dismissed with a shrug).

There is no more self-righteously, high-mindedly closed a mind than that of a nonconformist. It is likely that he will begin every conversation with some such gambit as "I know this isn't a popular position, but . . ." He will insist that no one since Galileo or Joan of Arc has had as much courage as he. Challenge him, and he will dismiss you as a peasant not worth his attention. "If you don't know what's wrong with American culture," I heard one champion nonconformist say down his nose to someone who mildly differed on the subject, "then there's no point even talking with you." You can never ask about the emperor's clothes lest you prove at once in the nonconformist's eyes to be a monumental repository of naïveté.

Obviously, neither conformity nor nonconformity is to be accepted or rejected per se. What is to be rejected is the nonconformity that is so sure it is right that it is going to cram itself down your throat. No doubt the heresy of today may well become the orthodoxy of tomorrow, but we should not hurry the process any more than we have to; heresies of worth are quite capable of making their own way.

If we have anything to fear from the conformists who wish to change the world in accordance with their ideologies, as we no doubt do, then we have equally much to fear from the phalanxes of the nonconformists—and perhaps more, for I sense an aggressive belligerence among nonconformist sects that seems as zealous as olden W.C.T.U. fanaticism. I am thinking, for example, of the San Francisco howlers for whom anything conventional is to be denigrated for the reason of conventionality alone. (Allen Ginsberg is a good example here, especially since as a talented poet, he might be expected not to follow easy patterns.) There are also those chronic nonconformists who do not have even a principle to guide them; they rebel in every direction at once for the sheer sake of perverseness. College campuses have become populated lately with bearded, anarchic mediocrities who blackmail their fellows and their professors into accepting them for more than their worth by trading on the current high value of nonconformity.

Nonconformism today, whatever particular form it takes, appears to be a legitimate enough descendant of the soft liberalism of the thirties. Like the Stalinist creed with which it was often allied, this liberalism saw the world through glasses that never quite focused on things in themselves. It saw things only as fuzzy abstractions that fitted a variety of inflexible needs of the mind. I recall the argument, for instance, that "decent" people were simply not aware of ethnic differences. An ingredient, too, of this soft liberalism was that puritanism which has always been a part of American intellectual life. It is inclined, a priori, to deny any pleasures or successes in popular culture and to look for its satisfactions in more rarefied atmospheres. (American movies have only recently been a subject for serious nonconformist discussion.) I suppose, too, that mass production, which was invading every aspect of American life in the twenties and the thirties, had to be resisted by a determined seeking-out and idealizing of the unique, the handmade product or thought.

One would have expected, however, or at least hoped, that the impulses that turned "thinking" persons away from the passive acceptance of mass-produced things and ideas would have also brought them to the enlightenment of approaching any thing or idea on its own merits rather than through a conditioned reflex. Certainly something like the Museum of Modern Art's tireless, wholesome independence in considering machine-produced objects as worthy of aesthetic attention should have helped nonconformism to develop more broadly, for the Museum is one of the worshiping places of New York nonconformists (although one should never underestimate the power of a nonconformist to compartmentalize). Certainly, too, one would have liked to think that nonconformism, once it cast off the shackles of Communist dogma, would not harden into similarly thoughtless patterns of response to fixed stimuli.

If nonconformity is to have its rightful say in American life, as it did with Emerson, Thoreau, Whitman, and Veblen, it must stop making a fetish of itself. Conformity, with its range of established, nonevangelical possibilities may, in the end, prove to have the greater attraction for those genuinely seeking a free and full life. After all, unrestricted amateur nonconformism is one of the honorable paths in American history. In the meanwhile, we must oppose all efforts of the dedicated nonconformists to make us nonconform according to their rules.

TWO

WONDERFUL TOWN?

New York, New York, it's a helluva town,
The Bronx is up and the Battery's down,
The People ride in a hole in the ground. . . .

NONCONFORMISM has two capitals, New York on the East coast, San Francisco on the West. New York, of course, is the older, the larger, the more dominant one. And it demonstrates particularly well the lengths to which nonconformist types will go to remain sheltered among their own.

The one thing even the most hardened New Yorker cannot avoid is the sheer presence of the city, its physical bulk, its complexities of movement, its squashing crowds, its oppression and indifference. Where Sherwood Anderson was the chronicler of small-town terrors, John Cheever today records metropolitan and suburban horrors. For cities exist by size, by forcing huge numbers of people through funnels into small areas, by neglecting utterly the eye's need and the body's need of nature, the mind's need for occasional separateness. Sooner or later, the plain difficulty of daily living—of getting from home to work and back again; of shopping; of going to the theatre, concert hall, or museum—makes anything the city may offer just not worth it. Only a whimsical arch-romanticist like E. B. White can after many years still address poems of adoration to the city, but then he has his Maine refuge.

Take New York. You can't get from any Long Island community into the city in much under an hour, and a quite uncomfortable one too, whether you drive through crowded traffic or bounce in a Long Island Railroad car or stand in the subway, lurching, elbows pinned, sweating, all the way to or from Jamaica or Flushing. I speak of Long Island, but it's the same for Westchester, Connecticut, New Jersey, Riverdale. That much publicized commuter's bus in Chicago with luxurious accommodations is just a desperate effort to do something about the problem; it would take a fleet of such buses, snarling traffic all the more, to take care of all Chicago commuters.

Return to the city? Before we left New York—never to return, we hope—such a movement was growing. Defeated, frustrated suburbanites were giving up their daily two-to-three-hour battle of attrition. They sold their split-level and ranch homes, took apartments at huge rents in the city, enrolled their children in private schools, disposed of their cars (or else settled down with them to that peculiar game adults play in New York, like musical chairs, of periodic daily shifting of parked automobiles). They accepted the lack of space, of greenery, of views of sky; the presence of smoke, soot, dirt, and noise.

But the worst thing these returning exiles accepted, I feel now, was a kind of living with the ever-present sense of the imminence of disaster. I am aware now, away from the city, of how casually one accepts sudden death in New York—the killing of a woman crossing Herald Square, her skull crumpled by a truck (I saw that); a plane hitting the Empire State Building (I worked across the street); the forcing of someone off a crowded subway platform into the path of a train (I used to look at daily headlines describing that; they said the person jumped or fell, but how could anyone ever know?); the falling of a flowerpot or a wooden beam from the heights of a building, to hit an old Negro man or kill a chauffeur in a Rolls-Royce (I read about these); and the countless daily acts of mayhem, so commonplace they never got into the newspapers. I remember two great winter strikes in New York in recent years that threatened disaster, one resulting in a shortage of milk, the other, of fuel. I remember, too, the shudder that swept the city when international politics seemed to be getting out of control and everyone became a private, momentary volunteer for Civil Defense, watching the skies for the plane that carried the little bomb. There was that occasional comic feeling, too, not unmixed with panic, of being jammed on Manhattan Island as in a Marx Brothers stateroom.

One accepts the nightmares of the city for the sake of culture, sophisticated society, jobs. As for the culture, during our last year in New York, my wife and I went to the theatre just once. That night cost us, with modest tickets, twenty dollars and several hours of nervous harassment. Even the museums and art galleries get intolerably crowded. Perhaps one can work harried and exhausted; it is more difficult to respond to art in that condition. Metropolitan social life and metropolitan jobs, too, once the enchantment wears off, become thoughtlessly competitive. Social caste becomes determined by work caste, and that, in turn, all too often, by one-upmanship. Insider-ism, snobbism, intrigue, become techniques of daily living. The most routine and essential services become marked by callousness: bus drivers ignore you in the rain; doctors and hospitals treat you as a moving cadaver on an assembly line. Anonymity is Everyman: as one must forget one's identity in the frantic motions at the beginning, middle, and end of the work day, so one forgets it in his office, at parties, with friends, even, at last, with his family and with himself.

Not everyone, of course, is lost, nor do all the lost lose themselves in the same way, but those that survive illustrate what it takes to stay alive and at what expense. I think of people I know who are not anonymous bodies in the big city. All are persons of the greatest self-understanding and independence of spirit and mind. But they, too, have clearly compromised with the demons; it is obvious that their work could be so much richer were they not required to spend so much of their resources countering the hazards of the city.

I know about the "cosmopolitanism" of New Yorkers. To me they are monstrous solipsists (as I was), with a built-in provincialism far narrower and more pernicious than anything found in the provinces. The urban area is their universe. In part, like any provincialism, this comes from innocence; in greater part, however, it is the result of the general competitive atmosphere: if one successfully bulls his way through the subway, through an office, through a cocktail shindig, through domestic difficulties, then the results *must* be worth it. If the game is worth the playing, it must be worth the winning. To some degree, every big-city dweller must be afflicted with this notion, else why does he remain? Why else does he allow himself to live in tenements, in an outrageous climate (there isn't a big city in this country today with a decent climate except San Francisco and Denver, which are really not "big cities" as Los Angeles and Chicago are), tied down to a job sometimes easily duplicated elsewhere?

The answer is that more and more he is breaking away. Sometimes reasons of health force him, against his will, to join the exodus; other times, retirement gives him an excuse for release; and some times, he flees in sudden awareness of the Kafkaesque bleakness. Relocation is becoming a national pastime, with more Americans living outside the state they were born in than ever before. It has become easier, even cheaper, to travel and to move one's household. The American family, as social workers and sociologists have been discovering with some surprise, has a built-in cohesiveness and stability it takes with it anywhere. The highways of the country are dotted with station wagons carrying families and pulling trailers. Cities and towns have become so much the same everywhere that one can pick up and leave home, school, church, shopping center, and a thousand miles away find everything duplicated. And if television has brought the glories of the big cities to the countryside at large, it has also brought that countryside into the big cities, one way or another. There is no longer a great unknown west of the Hudson or the Mississippi.

The big-city exodus is not unrelated to the growing sense of responsibility toward one's family. *Life* magazine reported on businessmen who retired young and moved their families away from the city to live in vacation territory, where they might spend more time with wives and children. There's a growing feeling that one just isn't doing right by one's offspring if the child isn't exposed to the countryside, some time, some way. Witness the boom in children's summer camps surrounding big cities. What makes more sense than to move the whole kit and caboodle to that countryside for all four seasons?

Artists, writers, free-floating intellectuals, who once made their way in droves to the big cities, are now finding small centers in congenial countryside which satisfy their longings. A Joseph Wood Krutch moves to Arizona; a Stanley Walker to Texas; a Leslie Fiedler to Montana; a Winfield Townley Scott to Santa Fe. And one suddenly realizes that writers have long functioned well removed from the big city: William Faulkner and Eudora Welty in Mississippi; Oliver La Farge, Ramon Sender in New Mexico; Walter van Tilburg Clark, until his recent move to California, in Nevada and Montana.

American cultural life which used to be centripetally focused on big cities is now becoming centrifugal. Advertising and business-administration college graduates may still head for New York or Chicago first, but scientists and engineers are spreading out. Young people interested in writing, painting, music, or just scholarship no longer find that they have to head for the metropolis. The state universities more and more are meeting local needs. One of the high-powered creative-writing college programs in the country is in Iowa, the heart of the corn belt that used to send so many young writers to Greenwich Village. The state universities of Ohio, Michigan, Wisconsin, Illinois are now foremost centers for study in the humanities. The University of New Mexico, in Albuquerque, sponsors a young artist for a summer of creative work at the D. H. Lawrence ranch in Taos, given by

Frieda Lawrence Ravagli to the University before her death. Frank Lloyd Wright had a major center for architectural thought and production in Arizona, at Taliesin West. Colonies of creative workers—of varying degrees of seriousness, to be sure—are to be found in the Carmel area of California, in Santa Fe and Taos in New Mexico, clustered about the many universities one finds in the climatically and scenically pleasing Far West and Southwest. Even persons who for one reason or another cannot break away completely from the big city try to reduce their dependence on it. Television and publishing personages in New York, for example, get out to the Connecticut woods or the Virginia hills and come to Manhattan only on business.

There is no real possibility, I suppose, of the big city's disappearing, or of its growing significantly smaller. But there is also no question, it seems to me, that the attractions once thought to be exclusive to the big city are now available in some form in the remotest areas of the country. Mencken has gone, and with him the definition of the hinterland as a cultural "Sahara." Artur Rubinstein, returning from a recent tour through that Sahara, commented: "Small towns throughout America are more receptive to fine music than old cities in France." Not only do small cities offer musical recitals of various sorts (I have just attended a concert of the Modern Jazz Quartet), symphony concerts, art exhibitions (including traveling displays from the big Eastern museums), theatre productions (unfortunately all too often imitative of Broadway box-office hits, although I have seen first-rate presentations of *The Devil's Disciple* and of Ionesco's *The Bald Soprano* in Albuquerque), opportunities for study and thought, but also all sorts of things big cities no longer offer, and in some cases never did offer—a relaxed pace of living, attractive physical setting, usually an authentic and as yet uncorrupted atmosphere, companions of the same stimulating type to be found in big cities and also companions of a type never to be found there. And you can *choose* among these offerings.

The small-city abominations Anderson, Lewis, and Mencken catalogued have all but disappeared as the result of greatly changed technology and sociology in American life since the twenties. Books and television are as ubiquitous as the latest enlightened theories of psychology, sociology, literature, history, and politics, broadcast far and wide by *Life,* Murrow, and Anchor Books. Privacy, if one wants that, is as available as in New York or Chicago, in some ways more available, for small cities tend not to become fragmented like big ones into neighborhoods and tenement communities, or into social cliques centering around one's job, with everyone jostling one another. The campus of the University of New Mexico is a freer and more relaxed place, intellectually more curious and open, than many institutions of higher learning in the metropolitan centers of the Midwest and East. Rotarians, Kiwanians, and Lions are all now "enlightened," and kid themselves—not least, to be sure, because of what Anderson, Mencken, and Lewis wrote. What many would consider the minimum essentials of civilization have spread everywhere: name a city of 100,000 or so, and it will surely have a first-rate restaurant offering a continental cuisine, a hi-fi shop, and a haberdashery discreetly advertising Ivy League suits and accessories. The big city is no longer the exclusive show place for the signs of wealth and urbanity.

Nor is the widespread enlightenment I speak of merely a matter of mass consumption of culture; creativity, I submit, is flourishing widely and significantly outside the city. It is true that writers, artists, musicians, thinkers cannot meet for lunch or drinks in the country at large as regularly and endlessly as in the cafés of Greenwich Village or Morningside Heights. But then, the work turned out today in the metropolitan centers alone is often of a rather special character and comes from a different impulse from the work produced elsewhere.

There was a time when artists had to borrow strength and assurance from one another, and the Chicago and New York salons were indispensable hothouses for cultivating talent, but today the soil is fertile almost anywhere but in the city, where it has become, at best, almost used up, at worst, poisoned. There is a nervous, frenetic quality about art exclusively manufactured in the city, in subject, tone, and achievement; it is focused narrowly inward; it springs as much from a badgering jealousy as from serious intention. (A friend, I learn, is to have a play produced on Broadway next year. I applaud him now and share unreservedly in his good fortune; a few years ago, in New York, my feelings would have been less generous, instinctively competitive.)

Creation must always be, even ultimately in the city, entirely personal and lonesome, indifferent to society. A Saul Bellow, a Bernard Malamud, a Herbert Gold, a Robert Creeley, a Leslie Fiedler, a Flannery O'Connor, a John Steinbeck, a Tennessee Williams, all move through the world at large, quite alone, and write.

As for that catalytic contact with personalities and ideas, always so important anywhere for productivity, one gets that at writers' conferences, with students (always stimulating and fresh in their responses and challenges), or with genuinely responsive people anywhere. Young writers used to complain to me that the togetherness of artists in the city had somehow crippled and sabotaged them; either they spent their time in interminable talk, evading their tasks; or the sirens of advertising, television, and publishing lured them away from their most serious purpose; or they fell into the easy and ready patterns established for them by dominant figures. The important idioms of our time have come from the lone artists, those geographically self-exiled from metropolis—Hemingway and Faulkner—or spiritually alienated from it—Cheever and Salinger.

Let me concede that the city always beckons, always lurks as the arena where the artist must submit himself to judgment. The city will always remain a place for occasional sojourn, where the artist can measure the response to his work and find out what is going on everywhere in his discipline. He carries on his routine business in the city and may even get himself recharged there, like a salesman attending a convention. But he does his solid work in the field, in the setting which provides an opportunity for a more authentic engagement with people, with ideas, and with oneself than most cities today can—in Jackson, Mississippi; on a Cuban island; in Santa Fe; in Majorca.

Subject, of course, to all sorts of exceptions and modifications, it seems easier to be eccentric, or to put it more happily, to be yourself, in a small city today amidst normal surroundings than in a big one. The most important thing smaller cities now almost alone offer in the United States is the one great thing it was thought in the twenties only the big city could offer (benighted metropolitan captives still think this)—a genuine chance to become most fully oneself, to carry out thought to serious conclusions, to develop meaningful relationships with family and friends, to work productively with one's best talents.

I was born, raised, and earned my living in New York, but the finest hour for me was when I picked up my hat and said, Farewell, my unlovely.

THREE

SAN FRANCISCO: THE WONDERFUL HOTHOUSE

THE BEST way, perhaps, to catch the spirit of San Francisco is quickly, floating through, in the course of a convention visit, say, or on a tourist-skimming. The distortion contributed by Martinis helps too. A longer and more sober settling-in would inevitably make the first glad impressions wisp away, and what was odd and curious and surely essential would blend with the ordinary and become familiar and normal. I floated through San Francisco one week in April in just this way, and I am sure I caught essences I never might have if I had stopped longer and for more ordered activities than those of a convention. I was able, also, in this condition, to catch that peculiar quality of the city which makes it with New York the co-capital of American nonconformism.

Floating may be the key word. You cross one of the two bridges into the city and feel as if they connect clouds, the clusters of towers and forested hillsides no more related to your roadway than they would be to an airplane. Below you, seemingly all around you, is silver, brilliant water, and in the distance, barely sketched in the haze, a delicate bridge connecting nothing. You top a hill in a cable car, and are plunged into a gasping view of city dropping like a precipice in front of you to water. I visited friends in Berkeley, across the bay. They have a back porch that thrusts into the air, like some rear observation platform on a huge stationary plane, and below you for miles you can see the clusters of Berkeley, Oakland, and even San Francisco, and the sheets of water distantly, blackly, melting into haze and horizon.

San Francisco is a city in the sky. In New York, Chicago, you are at the base of a canyon most of the time. There, the city surrounds you and tilts over you to keep out the sky. In San Francisco, you are on top of things, the sky surrounds you.

Even during the day, San Francisco has the air of a collection of posh side shows, piquant movie scenes, and dignified carnival rides. Elegant young gentlemen, in Ivy League suits, hats, shirts, and ties, clutching thin briefcases, gracefully swing onto passing cable cars, hang over the side while clutching a pole, and then gracefully alight with a short run before the car stops moving. A street in the center of town, closed to automobile traffic, has a series of shops and bars on each side that combine the most refined attempts at classiness of Fifth Avenue (especially the Park Plaza corner), Michigan Avenue in Chicago, and the boulevards of Paris and London: a building with no glass, its high façade entirely of brick in almost mosaic intricacy, with a tunnel-like entrance into a softly lit shop selling silver; a step-down pet shop with uniformed attendants, offering small palaces and tailored clothing for dogs and cats. You see young Oriental boys walking hand in hand with pretty Caucasian girls and vice versa, so often that you wonder whether miscegenation movies don't possibly puzzle San Franciscans. A neon sign on top of a building urges: "Don't Cremate Your Loved Ones, Calcify Them!" A circle of giggling Chinese children in the courtyard of the Reformed Buddhist Temple whirls happily around, while the shrill voices call out in a monotone: "Life is not worth living, life is not worth living!"

One afternoon, a refugee from my companions, I had lunch at Tiki Bob's, a bar which that week was offering a lingerie show during the noon hour with live models who paraded past your table. A tea garden, in Golden Gate Park, with Chinese arches and blossoming cherry trees, overlooks the Pacific, where again you have the sensation of floating. I had another lunch squatting on the floor of a Japanese restaurant, my shoes off.

The air during my visit was always balmy and golden, the brightness only slightly muted by the haze; I felt surrounded by towering palms and huge bushes with big waxy leaves and occasional pink blooms. Much of the time I was so surrounded. Once or twice I felt I was in a wonderful hothouse, enveloped in a marvelously delicate humidity, where all things were nourished to grow in the most grotesque individuality.

A three-day dipping into the newspapers is anthropologically invalid, no doubt, yet the impressions I got were consistent with other hasty ones. The full-page advertisements are slick and restrained with a lot of white, like those in the *New York Times* and in *The New Yorker*. The headlines inflate the barest events, like the *Daily News* and *Post* in New York. HOUSEWIVES AND COEDS IN PORNOGRAPHY RING, shouted one paper, but the story only remotely supported the headline. In the classified pages, "masseuses" advertise that they will come to your home "any time of day or night." It's still strange, for a former New York Giant fan, to read about San Francisco's baseball team. There was a flurry of headlines about the city being chosen for a summit meeting, all clearly arising out of speculation.

Feature stories exploit the city's cultural pioneering. A young psychiatrist announces the results of his census of the city's beatniks, among whom he lived for weeks ("100 days"): there are only 165 authentic beatniks in the city—that is, described by themselves as such as well as by at least two other self-designated beatniks. He gives the details of a mixed marriage, between a beatnik boy and a bourgeois girl, and reports solemnly that the boy shaved, washed, dressed, and got a job.

At night, of course, after a long cocktail party and wine with your Basque meal and an after-dinner drink, the town is a surrealistic fantasia. Friends took me pub-crawling. I met them at the Coexistence Bagel Shop, where the beatniks go for bagel and beer and sneering; we went to The Cellar for a poetry-and-jazz session; we stopped at a club where the performers, including a petite soprano and a Sophie Tucker type, were not females; we passed up The Purple Onion and The Spaghetti Factory and ended at the Hungry i.

Another night, with another group, I wended my way by cable car to Fisherman's Wharf, exchanging jokes about psychiatrists with the cable man (a convention of "orthopsychiatrists" had just ended), talking freely with persons who hopped on and off along the route. At the end of the line, we helped turn the car around on its turn-table ("More fun than Disneyland," one man remarked), and went for dinner to a place across from DiMaggio's, looking out through huge windows at rows of sailing vessels parked alongside the wharf like so many cars.

One surely doesn't live this way every day in San Francisco, not all day long, and doing all these things. At least, I would think not. Yet, a detached and remote reminiscence brings out the affectation of all this, and I wonder whether my enchanted routine isn't a common one for San Franciscans. It's an odd affectation, for unlike the same sort of thing in New Orleans, say, or Los Angeles, it's an affectation intended to take in not only the tourists, but to take in the natives and residents too, perhaps them especially.

In the North Beach area, the bohemian stronghold, one bar advertised in its windows two complete beatnik outfits. The "senior" one, for $6.95, had a black turtleneck shirt, black glasses, thong sandals, and a rope for a belt; the "junior" one, for three dollars, had the black glasses and the rope belt. While this may have been whimsy (with a bludgeon), several of the types within were actually uniformed in parts of these outfits, including a long-haired, solemn-mouthed girl sitting in an enclosure woven of fibre that looked like a huge bassinet turned on one end.

In the City Lights Bookstore (Ferlinghetti's emporium which published Allen Ginsberg's *Howl* and sells only paperbacks), I overheard a wispy bearded, burlap-shirted Oriental gentleman talking with a friend about the difficulties of getting a baby-sitter. Shades of bourgeois suburbia! Outside the bookstore, two unkempt young ladies passed, and one remarked about a pair of boys following them in a jalopy, "He looks like a dago. I'd like to be loved by a dago tonight." Juvenile delinquents with a script writer.

One dive had a huge sign on a wall giving the history

of the bagel and describing the process of making it (leaving out, incidentally, the essential step of boiling the dough). It's not enough to eat of the bagel ritualistically; the mystique requires you to know the bagel formula, however inaccurately.

Even the nightclubs were solemn, self-conscious. In The Cellar, while the young man was booming out (most effectively, I must report) his own and Auden's poetry to the heavy jazz accompaniment, principally of the bass, the audience sat attentively, hands folded, in a reverential paralysis, not talking, not flirting, not squirming, not even drinking the obligatory bottle of beer in front of them. No college student, no church-goer, could be more respectful. (But throughout there was the wonderfully honest, jeering, supercilious smirk of the bass player.) There couldn't have been many tourists in the place, for the poetry-cum-jazz affairs had dwindled to one night a week when I was there, and I found out about this one by chance from the local jazz grapevine.

At the Hungry i, there are no tables as in the Greenwich Village counterparts; you sit in rows of folding yacht chairs, your drink on the narrow arm, members of a Carnegie Hall-type audience, come to hear artists. Which is certainly fine, for the performers I heard deserved to be attended to (as does Mort Sahl, whose home base is the Hungry i), but it was the oddest nightclub I ever visited. Not even folksingers and former opera stars command such a pure attentiveness in New York or Chicago or Los Angeles. It wasn't the nightclubbing that mattered to the audience so much as the character of the place. Everyone seemed to feel he had a part to play in the city, from the cable car operators to the nightclub waiters, one of whom gratuitously confided some gossip to us about the performers.

And why not? San Francisco is an implausibly spectacular city, never letting you forget the glories of sea and sky and sun, for much of the year embracing you with a serene, delicate climate, right through the night. It would take someone with almost inhuman insensitivity not to respond to the physical glory of the setting. You have to spend very little time fighting the elements or the arrangements for commuting, working, shopping, general living. In spite of yourself, as in Paris, you are encouraged by the genius of the place to cultivate your uniqueness, to invent a uniqueness if need be, to learn it in school as a last resort (a creative writing seminar at San Francisco State College once enrolled 125).

The avant-garde of every kind can sprout and flourish here luxuriantly—perhaps too luxuriantly, with too little challenge to provide salutary tensions. I understand that more paperbacks of the most esoteric types are sold per capita in the Bay area than anywhere else. I was told also that there are more suicides per capita in the Bay area than anywhere in the world although a sociologist friend assured me that this was a statistical manipulation: there are just as many suicides in the Bay area as anywhere.

As I say, it's best to get the tones and the tastes of San Francisco fast, in passing; otherwise I would guess they may get stale and ordinary and depressing, like the third day at Disneyland.

FOUR

WONDERFUL COUNTRY

THE IMAGE the professional nonconformist has of the rest of the country is not a pleasant one. Since he is likely to be a lifelong resident of a large city, he is sure that he lives at the center of the universe; everything else must be wasteland. The countryside is thought of in easy visual pictures: stretching flatness, steaming valleys, slag-heaps of mountains. And he is likely to have these mental scenes confirmed by his short, occasional ventures out of the bosom of his city—south and east out of Chicago, say; any direction out of New York; east out of Los Angeles.

Small towns are thought of as prisons; their populations, captives straining for the freedom of the big city. Sherwood Anderson, Sinclair Lewis, F. Scott Fitzgerald, William Faulkner, have fixed in our minds so detailed, so pervading a sense of the meanness, pettiness, dullness, unimaginativeness, sheer horror, of the lives and values of the small town, that it is next to impossible, even with our own experience as evidence to the contrary, to modify this picture. And, of course, there is always some evidence to confirm the bleakness of the traditional portrait.

The residents of small towns themselves support this image. They are always making demeaning comparisons of their possessions with the glories of the large places; they apologize to visitors and to themselves. Even when they are perfectly content, their expressions sound like sour grapes, for their satisfaction is couched negatively: who needs the big city anyway? And the movement of population in the United States does happen to be from smaller to larger cities. Relatively few persons abandon the certain glories of the large city for the lesser and dubious ones of a small one except, as I have said, under the pressures of changing or transferring a job, or of the demands of health.

There is a context for carrying on discussions about the city and the country, a collection of attitudes and assumptions, even a vocabulary. It is taken for granted that if we know the troubles of big-city living, we also know the pleasures; if we know the shortcomings of the country at large, we also know the picturesque spots, the enchanting native haunts, the out-of-the-way corners. "It's a great place to visit, but I wouldn't want to live there." We even connect advocacy of the urban satisfactions with a political slant (liberalism); with a general sophistication; with a taste in clothes, literature, art, food, the sumptuary delights generally (we have the word "urbanity" to affirm this taste, and the supporting documents from Lamb and E. B. White, the "romanticists" of the city). The large cities are assumed to be the breeding spots for everything fine in the way of independence and nonconformity; only in the city can one practice beatnikism and other forms of bohemianism without having to answer to stuffy, narrow-minded bourgeoisie. American nonconformists once wandered the countryside, excluding nothing and no one—Whitman, Emerson, Thoreau; today, they wander the narrow streets of the slum sections of big cities and make pilgrimages from one metropolitan shrine to another, keeping their vision and their sensibilities carefully shielded from contamination with the countryside.

Yet if any of us tend to be glib about the virtue of the big city and the vices of the rest of the country, it is equally tempting to fall into the easy and sentimental defenses, no less glib, of our various regionalists, the champions of the Southwest, of the Florida keys, of the Monterey coast, of the Colorado hills. Occasionally it almost seems as if one has to justify himself, not only in the books he reads, the foods he eats, the clothes he wears, but in terms of the countryside he lives in. We hesitate to betray a love of the country, or a loathing of the city, lest we give away our true status; we find the prevailing tone for talking about a place and use it. And often, this tone, developed to meet all sorts of needs, is not altogether wrong; San Francisco, the Southwest, Cape Cod, the Vermont country, do deserve panegyric. But panegyric, like philippic, tends to be unmodulated and unqualified.

For the fact is that, romantic or sentimental as one might like to be about the country at large, the great debunkers of small-town life, who always used the big city as their vantage point, as the basis for comparison, were in large measure right. Small towns, small cities, are often indeed barren—barren of thought, of feeling, of large and generous responses to the world outside and to strangers. Small towns do tend to be xenophobic. The newspapers are provincial; local problems receive the same emphasis as international ones (when the latter are reported at all); editors proudly parade the lowbrow character of their tastes and opinions.

It is not fair or meaningful, however, to compare the small town of the twenties with the small town of today. In the twenties, the towns that Lewis, Anderson, Fitzgerald fled from were fixed in their arrangements of status and relationship; there was little flow into the society of new families, and except for the rebellious young people, there was little emigration out of it. Today, of course, mobility is a fact of our lives, with companies shifting personnel around freely, with families on the constant move to find a better job, better climate, better opportunities of every sort.

But while the newcomer will be received more cordially into the local closed community, this is only the initial gesture, almost part of a welcoming sales talk to join PTA, Rotary, Kiwanis, the local ladies' clubs, the Brownies, Cub Scouts, the church, the synagogue. After these early overtures, the newcomer is expected to know and accept the landscape and to have his own specific, defined place in it. Exclusion from the "proper circles" is sometimes no less rigid these days, but generally it's not an exclusion simply of the newcomer, the Jew, or the Catholic, but of the eccentric. The welcome mat is always out for anyone who wants to change his mind.

It is easy to mistake the early generosity with which one is greeted in a new community for a genuine and principled openness of mind and heart. When we first came to Albuquerque and for a number of years afterward, I found most pleasant what I thought was simply a largeness of understanding. I attributed the tolerance of oddballs to "the pioneer" spirit of the Southwest, which, I thought, still judged persons according to their deepest and most genuine qualities and not by mannerisms, origin, background, religion, details of speech. No doubt much of what I saw was a suspension of judgment, a suspension that would have been rare in the more competitive settings of big cities, where definitions and conclusions have to be made quickly and firmly. But much of it was simply a matter of suffering fools gladly, of not troubling to make evaluations, of not exercising distinctions and standards, occasionally even of hoping to attract the fool to one's particular club.

There is much "tolerance" in small cities today, tolerance between religious denominations, even between factions of the same denomination (Conservative and Reform Jews proudly announce their "brotherhood"), and even between Democrats and Republicans. Everyone is expected to be a good fellow. But this is not a tolerance that comes out of good-heartedness or a breadth of vision; it comes from indifference to fundamental issues. Religion, like politics, has become trivial, not a basis for a strong stand.

It is true, too, that one cannot hide from oneself so easily in smaller cities. Large cities offer one the illusion of depths and unknown territories in the variety of enchantments and escapes; you can lose yourself in dozens of museums, movie houses, theatres, concert halls, television programs, bars, cocktail parties, dinners, lunches, weekend drives, picnics, lectures, baseball games, beaches, adult-education courses, nearby resorts. It almost seems as though your own resources are endless. In small cities, one must cultivate the more delicate, the rarer, the lonelier recreations, reading, conversation, the local scenery, recordings; there are only so many places to go, people to meet, things to do.

What is merely an accident of population becomes a principle of life: the possibilities for stimulation, for response, for awareness, for thinking, are indeed fewer in small cities: life is more meager. But this is a truism, of course. Neither in the big city nor in the small—San Francisco or Ames, Iowa; New York or Albuquerque; Chicago or San Antonio—must one be limited by context.

The person who lives in the country does have one great advantage over the city dweller. The city dweller is often there as a matter of principle; that principle commits him not only to a point of view, but to a way of life in all of its tiny manifestations. In spite of all the possibilities for levels and varieties of experience, the city dweller moves in small habitual circles. Often he almost literally cuts himself off from unknown territory. He is geographically tethered. The editor of a national weekly, with headquarters in a large cosmopolitan center, once commiserated with me. "Don't you feel constricted living in Albuquerque?" he asked. I told him sometimes, but that I was endlessly busy at the university where I work, with reading, with my family, and with traveling around the country. "Ah, traveling," he replied, "I never get away. Do you really move around much?" I assured him I did.

Moving about, once the shell of the big city is broken out of, is natural in the country at large. Everyone moves about, often pointlessly of course, but never so pointlessly as big-city dwellers, racing on freeways, day-in-day-out. There is country to be seen, people to meet, towns to wander about.

For the United States is indeed a land of wonders, a wonderful country. The city offers the pleasures of the mind, of the sophisticated senses; the city is the center of civilization. The country offers unrestricted pleasures, the cultivation of responses to landscape and distance; it offers the bucolic and the pastoral. There is no country on earth like ours with a network of roads and railroads that bring one to so many natural wonders so easily.

Seeing the American landscape is nothing at all like seeing the European. Our wonders here involve principally the works of nature. But always, as anywhere, it is our sense of relationship to the scene that provides the stimulation and the satisfaction. In the soft contours of the Vermont or New York hills, we feel a calmness and an ease; the meadows are to be walked through, the hills to be climbed. The jutting, craggy peaks in Colorado subdue us; they are to be transgressed only with special equipment, after the development of special skills. The Ohio and Iowa countryside of lush, green, rolling plains and forests evokes history, satisfies the expectations of the familiar and ordinary, offers a sense of rest in itself and in its opportunity. We are lost in time and space on the edge of the Grand Canyon, lost in sculptured dreams in Carlsbad Caverns, lost on the moon in the Petrified Forest. The desert mocks: fire-hot, knife-sharp, it plays with color, variations on the theme of red-brown; it dots itself with contorted plants; it stretches away to dainty blue sky, to heavily purpled mountain.

Nor are the wonders of America only nature's: man's technological works are here to be wondered at, responded to: works done with nature, against nature, in spite of nature. Ancient man with his mud-built cliff tenements on the sides of the sheer hills in Mesa Verde and Bandelier; his descendants in the pueblos along the Rio Grande, using the same materials, the same architecture. Modern man with his mountains of poured concrete, backing up the Colorado River (which itself cut—and still cuts—the Grand Canyon), forming a huge lake, and sending electricity across the jagged mountains hundreds of miles, carried by steel, strut-limbed giants standing on mountainside, on desert, tilted, horizontal, in parade-straight lines, striding purposefully to the big ocean city.

There are the people to see and even to meet. In the Taos Pueblo I once got lost in a back street and came upon a group of Indian girls and women making an oven. One girl of high-school age was in the center of the rising circle of mud; the others were on the outside, including a thin, bent-over, thin-haired crone. The black mud spattered their clothes and their brown faces. They saw me, but before I could ask how to get back to the main plaza, they burst into derisive giggles, never once looking at me except sideways, and I fled. In Iowa, we wandered through the Amana cluster of towns, built by German religious settlers; in Utah, we stopped in Mormon country to see a local parade celebrating the first coming of the Mormons. We made no contacts at these places, but over the morning communal bathroom sink in the Grand Canyon auto camp, brushing their teeth, my wife and a young lady from Arizona met, and this resulted in a visit to a Hollywood screen writer and publicity man. In Bryce National Park, an area where weather eroded the red earth into razor-backed ridges bordered by valleys of towering chesslike figures (in clusters, with names like "Garden of the Gods"), a sales executive from Chicago taught me how to drive fast on the winding road which bordered sheer drops.

Irony and idiocy intrigue and bemuse one everywhere.

At Plymouth Rock, a guide in full Pilgrim outfit delivered a mechanical spiel, full of references to the spiritual dedication and selfless courage of the Mayflower passengers. It concluded with a request for contributions to pay him for his work. A crew of Hopi Indians, remote in their hauteur, splendid in their costume, picked up butts and papers all day in a national park and in the evening, before a campfire, did a dignified religious dance for the visitors—and promptly passed the hat. Along the Massachusetts coast we saw a billboard for a hotel called something like "The Pilgrim Inn." It showed a toothy, busty, long-legged girl in black net stockings, with a tiny Puritan-type apron and hat. "All the pleasures your heart desires!" the sign proclaimed.

But wandering gives no sense of place; the scenes, the encounters, add up, no doubt, a montage series of film clips. But America really is not a succession of scenes, flashed on and off the screen, although this may well be as much as we can ever expect: living in one setting long enough to apprehend the place may stale one for the character of other settings. America is a mosaic which one can never see whole, for we live on one or another of the fragments; yet we can make reports, send letters from our particular locales, record the local climate and geography. Indeed, with moving about comes a sense of what is not genuine; we learn quickly to respond to what is autochthonous and what imported; we catch the sound of affectation quickly.

America specializes in regionalism. Vermont has so insistent a modern folklore it is almost like Texas in this respect. New Hampshire, separated not even by a river from Vermont, as New York is, is considered in Vermont alien land. (When the farmer whose house was near the border was told that a survey had relocated him in Vermont, he remarked: "Well, I never did like New Hampshire winters.") Vermont barns and one-room schools are converted to sumptuous, modern houses, as are neat small brick buildings, all proudly designated as circa 1800. A local grocer at a lonely crossroad sells the only cheese of its kind in the world, made with scallions.

In Shelburne, Vermont, well inland, are an old schoolhouse, a jail, a farmhouse, a lighthouse from the center of Lake Champlain, rebuilt, stone by stone, plank by plank, each numbered and indexed, the whole process gloatingly described. The lighthouse overlooks a luxurious lake steamer itself, dragged cross-country and deposited in a meadow, just below the eminence of the lighthouse. As in Williamsburg, Virginia, the past is pickled in Shelburne simply as past, simply for antiquity's sake: art, esthetics, are incidental—not rejected, just ignored; but not simply for any old antiquity's sake, for the sake of the specific Vermont antiquity. Regionalism of this sort creates an attic jumble, a time machine out of control, zigzagging wildly across the past.

In Virginia, in the flat plains, is Williamsburg, which is a more carefully, more lavishly authenticated reconstruction, whose point perhaps goes beyond mere antiquarianism. The streets, the homes, the shops, the public buildings—the Governor's Palace, the House of Burgesses—are guaranteed to be original or faithful reproductions: the thick, blurring window panes in the House of Burgesses were specially made, we are assured, by the same processes as the original windowpanes of the eighteenth century. And did the modern glaziers wear the tricorn hat, knee breeches, and silver-buckled shoes? The bakers in Williamsburg dress in this fashion, as do the printer (wearing a kerchief over his head in pirate fashion), the wig-maker, and the pharmacist. The ladies who guide one graciously through the Governor's Palace, graciously asking that the original wall-paper patches not be touched, wear the billowing skirts of the eighteenth century, and march out, at the end of the day, through the governor's formal gardens, to their late-model sedans and station wagons.

In the Southwest and in the Rocky Mountain states, cowboy hats, cowboy boots, bolo ties, fiesta dresses, Spanish phrases set the regional tone. I am assured that the boots are not an affectation, that they are exceedingly comfortable, even for office wear or automobile driving; the hats a shield against the sun. Perhaps this is so, but why the defensiveness? We all want to belong, and it is so easy to make a gesture, to utter a word, in the ritual of belonging. These are charming details and so long as they remain private, they remain harmless. (During the founding celebration of Albuquerque, the Junior Chamber of Commerce threatened to put in stocks any man who didn't have a beard.)

Regionalism has to be huckstered, however; what is awful is that the shoddy gets mixed up with the genuine. But the paradox is that the white man's ingredient, the addition of his taste and business acumen, often improves things—perhaps as often as it destroys them. Zuni turquoise jewelry made for the white man's market is often more delicate, more finely worked, than the huge, bold, flamboyant pieces the Indians make for themselves: check the items put up for pawn at any Indian trader's post and compare them with those specifically made for sale to knowing whites. The best pottery, like that of Maria of San Ildefonso, has received acclaim through the white man's appreciation and efforts. But there is a line of Navajo rugs, quickly woven and cast into a pile, for the tourist trade only, coarse and blaring, a pole away from the subtle design and coloring of the genuine stuff.

It happens that my own region now is the Southwest; I live and work in Albuquerque. This is an area peculiarly rich in local color, juxtaposing and blending the Indian, the Spanish, and the Anglo, and I have been charmed by much of it. Cynics and smart alecks like to point out that the "native" Mexican food served in the Old Town restaurants is neither native nor Mexican; that most of the beams one sees jutting from the flat-roofed pueblo-style buildings are just stuck in from the outside. But I shall continue to like my occasional meal in Old Town; the preparations are indeed not Mexican and only remotely "local," but the concoctions are sufficiently original and valid to please me (including *sopaipilla*, a blown-up, hollow, doughy confection, crisp brown, into which one pours honey, and which one eats like a slice of bread or a tortilla with the hot meal).

I shall continue to think buildings styled like the United Nations Secretariat outlandish in the desert. By far the most charming buildings in the city are the pueblo-styled structures on the University of New Mexico campus. They may not be built of adobe and may exceed, here and there, the height of the Taos tenement pueblo, but they please the eye, for their proportions are neat, the occasional carved decorations handsome, and they fit into the landscape.

The land calls for conformity. The Pueblo Indians realize this; each tribe is like one person. Pueblo children in school do not know how to compete; they blend in with the whole class; they have identity only as members of a group. The Pueblos maintain their character as Indians only to the extent that they continue to conform to the ways of their tribe. And an inevitable paradox emerges: the most fiercely unassimilable groups contain the most uncompromisingly conforming individuals.

I wonder, too, whether the mystique of the land does not extend to the Anglo settlers. The persons I have met, in Albuquerque and in Santa Fe, who are the most insistent on making their own way, have also adopted local customs on a large scale: one lives in a rambling adobe structure; another wears bolo ties; another will not miss his daily canter over the countryside. Some are almost corny in their conformity.

Conformity, one recognizes in the New Mexico landscape, is not a way of denying individuality; it is a way of asserting it. One is never free, it is obvious, except when acknowledging the limitations of reality, accepting what is congenial in any given context, separating the trivial from the meaningful. To be oneself anywhere, it seems necessary to be able to take for granted one's roots, one's place in a community. Of course, accommodations are necessary: the terrain will insist on asserting its own nature. But I think of desert plants. In desert soil, the piñon tree sinks a twisting mass of clutching roots, reaching out widely for nourishment; on wetter mountainside, the root system is less elaborate, less tortured. On desert and on mountain, the gnarled piñons are exercises in contorted individuality.

FIVE

AMERICAN BUSINESS AND NONCONFORMITY

ONE OF the major problems affecting American business and industry today is an intangible one, a social and psychological one, the matter of conformity and nonconformity. It is possibly even more serious than some of the classical problems, for we have by this time worked out elaborate theories and approaches to deal with supply and demand, say, or buying power, or inflation. We have few answers, not even confused ones, to the question of conformity, which affects business and industry profoundly, both on the inside and on the outside. Indeed, except for tentative and uncertain probings here and there, like Whyte's *Organization Man*, the broad implications and effects of the nonconformity issue in the areas of business and industry are scarcely acknowledged, at least in any conscious and open way.

It is not that American industry is oblivious to the question. What seems to have happened is that by and large industry has tended to take its critics' view of it when considering the problem at all. American capitalism —the very word is enough to make one shudder, such has been our conditioning—is looked upon and looks upon itself as the citadel of conservatism, conformism, stuffiness, resistance to progress and new ideas of any sort. This is at best. At worst, it is conceived of as narrow, vulgar, unethical, always treading the edge of illegality and immorality. The popular myth pictures the American businessman as much more like Babbitt or George Washington Hill than like Silas Lapham or Dodsworth. Indeed, in spite of the mountainous evidence to the contrary, this image of himself may well be the one held by the typical successful businessman, when he bothers to think of the matter at all. This is borne out by Joseph W. Maguire's article in the July–August (1960) number of the *Harvard Business Review*, which reported that a survey of bankers showed that, by and large, they accept the standard image of businessmen portrayed in Lewis' *Babbitt*, Marquand's *Point of No Return*, Whyte's *Organization Man*, and Hawley's *Executive Suite*. One can understand this: the capitalist's preoccupation is not with appearances but with accomplishments; it is easier to accept a ready stereotype, no matter by whom created or for what reason, than to bother about a more modulated true image. Yet it is one thing to paint in all the warts, as Cromwell asked; it is certainly another, as is being done constantly in portraits of Americans, to paint only the warts.

The question of nonconformity may well be argued to be at the heart of the American economic system, as it is, for that matter, of our entire social structure. From the earliest days of our colonizing and pioneering to the days of the great immigrating, nonconformists laid down the new patterns of development. Nonconformists broke through expected and easy lines of behavior and response. The Kit Carsons and Daniel Boones of our geographic frontiers are matched by the Astors, Vanderbilts, Rockefellers, Fords, Morgans, Gimbels, Strausses, of our industrial, financial, commercial frontiers. We need not belabor this point, certainly; it is one of the tarnished commonplaces of American business history, so tarnished, actually, that we sometimes miss its true shine.

We tend to overlook our great tradition of nonconformity (or "independence" or "individuality" or "radicalism," call it what you will; in essence, the principle is nonconformity) for the simple reason that our solitary men, the pioneers, have always been followed by the hordes of conformists. It is the way of conformity that seems to so many, here and abroad, to be our more natural way. If we beat our way to the door of the man who builds a better mouse trap, we also beat it to the doors of his multitude of imitators. And I would argue that this is of the peculiar nature of the American genius: a man has a dream; it turns out to be practical, that is, to be good for many persons; it is adapted to the assembly line —so that everyone can enjoy the dream. The dream moves inevitably from nonconformity, the small domain of the purest individualist, to conformity, the territory of the many.

No better example of the mixture of intransigent, uncompromising nonconformity mixed with a stubborn conformity can be found than in the career of Henry Ford. He broke through every engineering, financial, and production barrier fencing him in as he moved from dream to reality. In American industrial history, Ford is perhaps the most cantankerous of the princes of nonconformity. But as we all know, it was also he who established the symbol of conformity for the contemporary world: the assembly-line turning out identical products, never varying in components or in color. The man who saw his problems with a uniqueness rare in our world, as though they had never existed for anyone else but himself, would allow his customers, whose needs and wishes he shrewdly recognized, to have only black cars.

My point is simply this: that without the principles implied in conformity—the recognition of widespread common wishes, in short, the recognition that people do feel and think alike in very many areas and want very similar things; the application of the efficiency and economy inherent in mass production, distribution, and advertising—our society could never effectively make available the products of nonconformity. Indeed, without the comforts and conveniences implicit in an assembly-line culture, without the commodities of conformity, from miracle dishwashers to miracle drugs, from exotic liqueurs and espresso coffee to hi-fi components, Americans could never so effectively explore their uniqueness as individuals. They would not even have the things with which to be nonconformists: they would not have cars or boats "to get away from it all," they would not have the hi-fi sets to listen to obscure music. The assembly-line American culture which so many nonconformists deride gives them the wherewithal to be nonconformists, to have their leisure, to explore and exploit their differences.

We cannot emphasize enough the intimate connection in American life between conformity and nonconformity. General Electric is an industrial giant systematically employing all the forces and devices of conformity; it was also the company that sponsored Steinmetz and Langmuir in highly individualistic research. The American Telephone and Telegraph Company backs the most abstruse research into mathematics, much of which can only be fruitful to the degree that it breaks out of established patterns. I am not suggesting that G.E., or A.T. & T., or Du Pont, or Monsanto, or Dow, or Pfizer, or Westinghouse, or any other huge concern is being simply altruistic in its sponsorship of basic, nonconforming, non-"functional" research, or is conducting its research for reasons of "public relations." (Of course, many companies for various reasons are being altruistic and are aware of their public images in this area, recognizing the benefits to all society of such work, and thus ultimately to themselves, but in no specific way.) What I mean to say is that genuinely original research, the result of the nonconforming mind and talent, is understood by hard-headed, practical executives as being preliminary to mass-produced, conforming, widely satisfying products.

It may seem paradoxical at first to insist on the indissoluble link between nonconformity and conformity in this aspect of American life, yet what would there be to mass-produce, what new sections of the country would there be to settle with rows of identical houses with identical refrigerators, washing machines, and television sets, what movies and television shows would there be to see, what sorts of currently fashionable clothes would women have to wear—if it were not for the talent, inventiveness, daring, the unsentimental individuality of nonconformists in every nook and corner of our industrial civilization?

Consider for a moment the film and advertising industries as particularly piquant instances of the partnership between conformity and nonconformity. No one who has looked fairly at the products turned out on Madison Avenue and Hollywood can at one time or another but marvel at the ingenuity, the oddness, the steady exploitation of freshness (please note that I do not talk of art here, or even of originality, although I venture that the energies and talents devoted to mere freshness and uniqueness might well produce art if refocused) that have been put to the uses of conformism. Very few of the undiscriminating critics of American movies and advertising express themselves in language that is as precisely worked, as cunningly considered, as sensitively aware of the thin line between the pleasures of nonconformity and those of conformity.

It is precisely Hollywood which vividly illustrates the peculiar problems raised by the tensions between conformity and its opposite. While originality is recognized as essential to finding and introducing new elements in the movies, it is also recognized that following a trend, riding a wave, imitating and conforming, are perhaps even more essential in satisfying public demand. It is one thing, and a noble one, to inspire and elevate public demand; it is another to satisfy it. The public may be excited by a new type of movie, one which indeed offers a new perspective for an old subject—an adult Western, say; this is fine, but it wants more of the same, a lot more; it is not ready to receive something new immediately. *High Noon* achieved its success by not conforming to the ready pattern of cowboy movies; its imitators by the hundreds achieved their success by conforming to *its* pattern.

The same order of events applies to big industry. Why do automobile manufacturers follow one another so closely in their styles? Is it a simple matter of simple-minded conformism? History tells us otherwise. Early nonconforming automobile styles simply did not catch on: Chrysler came out in the thirties with a prematurely streamlined car; Buick in the forties had large window areas; Crosley and Willys and Kaiser all produced small cars. I cite these particular nonconforming innovations, for while they all failed to attract large enough followings at the time of introduction, *every one* of them is now in vogue. All the late-model cars are streamlined; all have vast window areas. And, indeed, the small foreign cars and the small American ones have become new symbols of conformism. The nonconformism of one period becomes the conformism of another.

There is no question that some of the peculiar horrors in the design of American commodities and buildings, the ones so often decried by our foreign and native critics, are the result of a thoughtless, mechanical, all-too-conforming adherence to nonconformist developments. The architectural style of the United Nations Secretariat or of the Lever Brothers Building, in New York, were moderately daring when first introduced and certainly had some point in trying to make most efficient and most attractive use of little space and to overcome a sense of crowdedness with height, great window space, and panoramic views; but what sense does a similar structure—a cigar box on its side, to use Lewis Mumford's phrase—the wide rectangles all glass—make in the middle of the desert? Why fins or gulls' wings on all our latest automobile models? Chrome is fine for protecting vital parts and edges of the exterior of a car; why slap it on anywhere and everywhere?

The point here, as elsewhere, is the need to distinguish what is truly necessary from what is not. It makes sense to criticize cars splattered with chrome lines and decorations that serve no functional or esthetic purpose; it makes no sense whatever to criticize kitchens outfitted with stainless steel appliances, as, for example, Louis Kronenberger has done, as though stainless steel, in and of itself, were one of the abominations of our culture. Stainless steel happens to be easier to keep clean, and it happens not to chip. Perhaps stainless steel is not to Kronenberger's esthetic taste; he may prefer black wrought iron. But the issue is not his taste or mine; the issue is, as I say, what a thing is for, and why.

I suppose I get as annoyed at seeing a baby's crib in the rear of a Volkswagen as any bearded sports-car aficionado gets while scanning a Detroit dinosaur. And, obviously, one of the new problems in selling cars Detroit has to contend with is this irrational, sometimes fanatical impulse of modern-day puritans, the crowds of habitual nonconformers, to abandon common sense and to betray their simplest needs. Of course, Detroit is not blameless in this new development, for there is no question, I think, that the designers who stretched out American cars far beyond the point of sense or comfort, who slapped the surfaces with dabs and lines of chrome like so many travel stickers, who increased the horsepower and the consequent expense with mad abandon, themselves helped accelerate the nonconformist reaction.

Within the private precincts of industry and business one can also see the unceasing tug of war between conformity and nonconformity. The organization man, the man in the gray flannel suit, the yes-man, the eternal joiner—all have become figures in our popular mythology of the mass conformity of executive personnel. Even making fun of this straw man, as Marquand does in *Sincerely, Willis Wayde*, and vigorously criticizing him as a heartless new criminal type, as in some recent television plays and novels, have become routine procedures among the gray flannel men themselves. In some way, one supposes, they think to remove the stigma of their conformity by joining the ridicule of and attacks on—no one else but themselves. They become as automatic no-men as they are yes-men.

While the large corporations will certainly continue to hire young executives to fit a certain mold, as a kind of insurance (after all, this model has proved itself), and will even investigate the wives of such young men to see that they fit into appropriate molds also, every top executive knows very well that except for the most routine and clerical jobs, it is the man of individuality, of real creativeness, of genuine imaginativeness, of bold nonconformity, who is needed to spark an organization into fruitful, meaningful activity. New blood is always welcomed, not simply a transfusion of undifferentiated old plasma from a blood bank. All the mass-produced types can do is repeat what has been done up to now; they cannot respond to shortcomings. They have been chosen to accept and be able to repeat; they are indeed interchangeable but only on an assembly line doing exactly the same thing as the man they interchange with; they cannot innovate, invent, create, imagine, think for themselves. And this is true of the professional nonconformist as well. All of these are guaranteed to conform according to prevailing rules.

Where, then, do the leaders come from? We have a paradox here that manages to resolve itself very effectively. With occasional and desperate exceptions, like Beatniks hired to pep up some advertising copy or manufacture new recordings, our new executives do come from within the ranks. They do happen to have that surface quality of being poured from a mold; some are even related to the boss. But the qualities necessary to get a job are often unrelated to those necessary to get ahead in one, and suddenly a gray flannel man detaches himself from the mass, becomes himself, and provides the invigorating new blood of nonconformity. Obviously the nonconformity that emerges from conformity, that is, the individual who rises from the ranks, to use a hallowed formulation, combines the new and the old, the radical with the traditional; he not only has branches that soar, he has roots as well. And of course the great problem of any executive who hires and promotes is being able to distinguish the potential nonconformist in the ranks of the conformists, to select the nonconforming face of the *man* among the gray flannel *dummies*.

There are many forces making for conformity in American life and militating against nonconformity. People simply want to do things together. Aside from the economy inherent in driving mass-produced cars, or wearing assembly-line clothes, there is also the wish to belong to a community whose ways and whose appearances are familiar and reassuring. Grow a beard, wear black stockings, forego lipstick and comb, but only so long as there are a few others who do the same. You can't jeer at the world all by yourself; you do need some company. It is very difficult to think of a nonconformist pattern that didn't achieve some degree of respectable conformity before dying out or becoming totally conformist. Our only true nonconformists have been, in the best sense of the word, "cranks," men with unflagging courage in their idiosyncrasies, like Franklin, Thoreau, Whitman, Edison, Frank Lloyd Wright, men who kept piling one idiosyncrasy on another. These are our honored "expatriates" in the very midst of our society.

It seems to me clear that neither conformity nor nonconformity can exist without the other, and I do not mean in terms of contrast, or for the sake of definition: the relation is symbiotic, each living off and nourishing the other. The dangers are that in an excess of one we may stifle or inhibit the other. The nonconformist who decries conformity is as much to be feared and resisted as the conformist who wants to eliminate nonconformity. But obviously nonconformity, which must always be the smaller and weaker, is in far greater danger from conformity, which is always larger and by its very nature better organized. The problem is maintaining a vigorous, healthy, positive, meaningful nonconformity in American life, supporting it, encouraging it, but never binding or restricting it, and never confusing true nonconformity with its fashionable imitation, mass-produced nonconformity.

For genuine nonconformity there must be a depth and breadth of background and understanding, and where else but in our schools can we get this depth and breadth? Yet it is in our high schools, colleges, and universities that conformity is being nurtured and nonconformity stifled. I do not mean in any simple and clear way, for in fact the keynote of American professional educators in our time is "individuality." By narrowing the curriculum to "practical" subjects, by reducing standards so that everyone may "succeed," by encouraging an atmosphere of "togetherness" regardless of fundamental differences among young people, students are being turned out who are hesitant about their uniqueness, who have little sense of the possibilities of human thought and achievement (they know little history or literature), who do not want to fly above or apart from the flock, but merely to blend with it as another speck.

Even a decade or two ago college graduates were sufficiently well prepared to move out in all directions; they were educated, not merely trained. A Dartmouth B. A. of my acquaintance has been, in order, a journalist, an editor, a negotiator for a labor union, the personnel director of a large company, their labor-relations specialist, and now the manager of a branch plant. Would most men with training primarily in business administration or engineering have the flexibility and built-in breadth to move about in this way? An engineer or a scientist without an education can rarely be more than a technician. A narrowly trained business-school graduate can rarely become an executive on any policy-making level. (Exceptions by the dozens may be cited, but these will, I am sure, generally prove my rule: the accountant who becomes president of a large corporation is usually a man of great natural resources and has, on his own or otherwise, developed that breadth and depth in human relations and background which comes with a solid liberal arts degree.)

The business world well recognizes all this when it puts a premium on a B. A. with good liberal grounding over a B. B. A. with the best training in business. But because we will always need bookkeepers, clerks, draftsmen, technical assistants of all sorts, who do require specialized if shallow training, the universities become confused and, sometimes without being aware of it, emphasize vocational preparation rather than education. And business conspires in this arrangement, by offering scholarships to narrowly delimited engineering specialists, for example. It would be the healthiest sign for our whole culture if American business and education established scholarships for achievement in liberal arts subjects and for evidences of genuine originality and individuality.

The American people respond too easily to slogans and

easy formulations. Business and industry have long been attacked by myopic and blindered critics as being the sources and the strongholds of conformism in this country. The labels of Babbittry, of Chamber-of-Commerce thinking, of Rotarianism have had just enough truth in them to become accepted widely as accurate evaluations. Yet in the most meaningful way possible, business and industry are freer than the campus, than politics, than any particular area of American life you wish to name, for in business the most wild-eyed nonconformist can, sooner or later, have his day if he proves himself in the impersonal arenas of production and marketing and competition. How long would a Howard Hughes survive on most campuses in this country? Or a Frank Lloyd Wright? Or indeed, a Henry Ford? I say "campus," for much criticism of American capitalism comes from the academies, but many other locales would serve as well. Perhaps the only enterprises in which the intellectual nonconformist can freely try his specialized wares are in literature or painting or music, and even here we can cite cases of nonacceptance, of active rejection, that are more gross than anything encountered in business.

What American society needs at this time in our cultural history, it seems to me, is not merely a more tolerant and discriminating sense of what is and what is not genuinely conformist, or nonconformist, but, far more urgently, an awareness of the interrelatedness of these two ways of life and thought. It is much too easy to find oneself seeming to defend one or the other, when in fact we are actually speaking for both. The nonconformist who speaks proudly of "our group of nonconformists" is only undercutting his own position, for as soon as you have more than one nonconformist, you have a movement, however small it may be, which would like to impose its ways on others, or simply assert the superiority of its ways over those of others. The staunchest conformists, on the other hand, who concede, however grudgingly, the compelling if occasional need for originality at once acknowledge the fundamental importance of nonconformity.

What business must do is balance delicately the opposing pulls of conformity and nonconformity, never in terms of abstractions or mere wishes or the most convincing of appearances, but on the basis of facts and reality. We cannot meaningfully live our personal lives always fleeing from ourselves, always finding a group with whose values and tastes and habits we may identify ourselves. No firm, no organization, will ever totally fulfill its potential if it does not recognize its uniqueness and the urgent need to maintain it. Even more than individuals, it is necessary for business and industry, within their own walls and in their relations with the public, to acknowledge the social, cultural, even psychological forces of conformity and nonconformity which affect their destiny, and to accommodate to them intelligently.

SIX

INSOLENT CRITICS, WONDERFUL CHARIOTS!

WHEN I was a boy in the 1920's, one of our favorite innocent diversions, along with trading cowboy cards, shooting immies, and memorizing out-of-state license plates, was exchanging car lore. It was a mild diversion then. Cars didn't change much from year to year. The Packard had the same front radiator, model after model; the Pierce-Arrow had the same headlights rising out of the front fenders. We knew pretty well, too, the insides: the six-, the eight-, and the twelve-cylinder jobs, as well as the four-cylinder ones. Everyone, our parents too, talked cars amiably, without lust and without fury.

All this is changed. My son has to learn each year's array of models from scratch, and has never really bothered to learn the foreign cars or the Cadillac vintages. He has abandoned the whole business. But it is among adults that we have a new syndrome—"automobile neurosis," or "car fever." It shows itself in two quite opposed ways. The common form is the sudden, irresistible impulse to own a new model, domestic or imported, compact or king-size, regardless of the good condition of one's present car or the lack of money. This affliction is more or less seasonal and apparently follows cycles, showing up every two or three years, according to a pattern not altogether figured out. With cars, as with some physical diseases, there are British, German, French, Italian, and even Japanese forms of the fever. It is not an altogether harmless affliction, but fortunately our economists, sociologists, and other students of the American social organism recognize its nature and keep working at cures.

Not so easily diagnosed is the form of the fever which expresses itself in a rage against cars, old and new, against Detroit, against chrome, against automobile upholstery, against new designs, etc., etc., etc. Auto buffs, who suffer from a galloping but really milder type of the neurosis, have various magazines to fuel their fever. The autophobes have a journal too. Every spring, they can rush out to read the automobile issue of Consumer's Union *Consumer Reports*, which may be relied on to describe, in delightfully nauseating detail, the new abominations of design and trim and confusions of function that mark the new crop. From time to time, the Reports will suggest to a car-hater, who will sooner use a pogo stick than drive a car bedecked with chrome, that he go to a little man in an alley and have the trim removed. This is a sort of undesigning of cars.

Autophobes hate cars for much the same collection of reasons they despise anything popular, but also for one or two special ones, having to do with the delights automobiles are supposed to promise. Most autophobes do not actually want to take an ax to all cars. The average autophobe has a soft spot for some particular model, usually a foreign make, with which he scornfully compares all other models. Sometimes he will even have a favorite among American cars. The old Lincoln Continental and the 1953 Plymouth are special objects of affection among autophobes.

Like other fanatics, most autophobes do start from a rational enough basis, shared by non-fanatics (there is much to be said against some American cars, after all), and then leap away toward the moon. Many, of course, have reservations about their positions and leave a way back for themselves to earth. Some even get over their autophobia suddenly, when the chips are down, and buy a despised American model, because they see they don't have the chips for a foreign car (whose illusory "low cost" is often the result only of comparison with models one would not think of buying anyhow; say, a Falcon or Rambler as compared with a "family" foreign car—a Peugeot or Mercedes-Benz or Jaguar sedan or even a Microbus, each of which will cost $500 to $2000 more—in which one can go cross-country comfortably with a wife, two kids, and some luggage). Autophobia, like autophilia, may even be thought of as in some ways a benignant condition, especially when the patient returns home before undergoing the shock treatment of a purchase. You usually develop resistance to succeeding infections; a couple of kicks at the tire, a peek under the hood, and you've had it. Autophobia is also a harmless enough way of stimulating the bile.

But occasionally a patient is afflicted with such a virulent form of the disease, embodying every classical manifestation, that a return to normalcy seems hopeless. These are fascinating clinical cases. Just as physicians learn much from studying medical pathology, so may we learn something from studying extreme autophobia.

We are fortunate in having a recent work that is a definitive anthology of all autophobic complaints, as well as all sorts of accompanying ones, John Keats' *The Insolent Chariots*. Mr. Keats hates car owners, car buyers, car salesmen, car dealers, car manufacturers, car designers, station wagons, convertibles, hard tops, super highways, non-super highways, service stations, Madison Avenue, psychologists, the Midwest, social scientists, the Far West (especially California), foam rubber, plastic, car ports (which he spells "Kar Ports"), split-level houses, big cities, small cities, chain stores, national brands, automatic transmissions, power steering, deodorants, suburban housing developments, tourists, Cape Cod natives, dirndls, shorts, and so on and on. He is, finally, contemptuous of the whole of America itself. This is a staggering performance and can only inspire awe. Mr. Keats starts with cars, which no one would begrudge him the good clean fun of ridiculing, and ends up by throwing away the whole shebang. In this, of course, he is at least consistently conforming to the nonconformist pattern.

It would be impossible and pointless to consider all or even a good number of Mr. Keats' objections to American cars. Some of them are highly whimsical and personal. He is unhappy, for example, that there are "nylon Karakul" rugs on the floors of luxury cars. He objects to the nylon; it should be real Karakul. But he also happens to object to rugs on the floors in the first place. He does, however, voice several widespread objections to American cars, held not only by autophobes but even by persons moderately neutral about Detroit. These objections are, of course, standard in all respectable nonconformist circles.

The design of automobiles infuriates Mr. Keats, as it does most nonconformists. "Execrable shape," he addresses the car. "If you happen to think the best form of anything," he writes, "is that which most closely fits the function to be served, you are being quite reasonable." This comment, of course, embodies not only a philosophy of style but a philosophy of life, and I shall come back to its full implications in a moment. Mr. Keats has no doubt at all that the form of the American automobile does not fit its function, and pursues this particular specter relentlessly. Complaints about automobile design, however valid, are highly tentative anyway, lending peculiar futility to Mr. Keats' abusive chase. Like complaints about women's fashions, they can be dealt with by waiting a year or so. It's as silly to harbor long a complaint about the New Look in cars as about the New Look in dresses.

But let's get back to the basic question: just what form of the automobile would indeed best fit its function? Just what is its function, for that matter? We can all agree that a car must have four wheels (perhaps only three for very small models), seats for the driver and some passengers, a place for the engine, a roof of some sort, doors, some carrying place. But after these basic needs of a car are met, design is pretty much a matter of free esthetic enterprise. I submit that variations of the shell, window space, doors, protective trim, are matters of taste finally and not of function.

Is the form of the Volkswagen, the only car to which Mr. Keats gives grudging approval, actually more suited to its function than the form of a conventional, "large" American sedan is to its? I think not. If you argue that the Volkswagen's smaller total size enables it to offer greater gasoline economy, I answer that its size is also related to the number of passengers and amount of luggage it can carry. A two-door American sedan can carry two more passengers than a Volkswagen as well as a good deal more luggage, and do both more comfortably over a longer distance. It consequently has a different function. Even the new compact American cars offer uses different from those offered by the Volkswagen or Dauphine. But this is not altogether what Keats and other autophobes have in mind when they attack American cars. They complain most vociferously about chrome trim that does not protect, or length that does not offer additional seating or luggage space, or plastic upholstery that looks like leather, and the like.

My sympathies, let me say at once, happen mostly to be with Keats here, but they are only my sympathies, that is to say, my feelings about the look of things. I happen to have developed a taste for unadorned, straightforward, unluxurious objects. I was raised in a time when modern architecture with its spare, hard, boxlike lines established itself not only as a way of building but as an ideology of life. Any form which did not sparely fit its function was anathematized as an example of ("Ugh! Horrors!") "conspicuous consumption."

But this is obviously only a personal and private response, however universal one might like to think the principle involved is. There are perfectly estimable persons who prefer furniture, buildings, automobiles that suggest the elegance of more expansive periods than the American Depression—the Victorian age, say, or the Renaissance. Mr. Keats and I happen not to like lavishly chromed cars, or cars that are longer than they have to be, but then other persons may like just this sort of thing, and the question has nothing to do with the interaction of form and function. Cars that gleam with chrome or approach buses in size still carry passengers inside (and sometimes, indeed, very comfortably).

If the function of a suit is as much to clothe a man as to please him (or does Mr. Keats wear burlap sacks?), or of a house as much to satisfy the occupants as to shelter them, why may not a car have the additional *function* of pleasing the owner as well as transporting him? It is not uncommon for us to sacrifice some degree of function and even of comfort for the sake of appearance, for the sake of an esthetic need (witness the return of the fireplace even to a Frank Lloyd Wright house), why may we not make such a sacrifice even in a car?

But putting the issue as one of taste would not satisfy any nonconformist, let alone so high-minded a one as Mr. Keats. Nonconformists would no more think of allowing such things to be resolved by individual taste than their ancestors, the Puritan witch-burners, would think of allowing matters of theology to be resolved by the individual conscience. It is evil, wicked, depraved to believe anything independently of what the self-appointed elders of the community declare to be gospel. It is especially horrid to follow a way of life that suggests luxury, self-indulgence, the pursuit of idle, "functionless" pleasures, satisfactions that momentarily please the eye or body. The hard and the uncomfortable are good: foam rubber is sneered at as a temptation of the devil. The violence of our seventeenth-century witch-burners is matched only by the moralistic fury of our twentieth-century hide-bound nonconformists. It is not enough for such persons themselves to boycott Detroit automobiles; they don't want anyone else to buy them either. Detroit, like drink, must be totally prohibited.

Mr. Keats aligns himself with the most constrictive and sour puritan tendencies in still another regard, his derision of the "sexual" suggestiveness he finds in automobile design. Like so many self-righteous and inconsistent nonconformists, Mr. Keats is so carried away by his frenzied argument, he accuses the automobile-makers of "anthropomorphizing" cars, building in all sorts of phallic, vaginal, bosom, and posterior images. He makes this complaint after he himself has called the cars "insolent chariots." As for myself, I find automobiles neither insolent nor voluptuous; they have never insulted me or whistled at me. Mr. Keats here simply confuses the feelings some observers have suggested that people have about their cars with the cars themselves. I suppose a determined enough Freudian could do an interesting analysis of Mr. Keats' own psyche: he expresses special antipathy both toward the phallically designed Thunderbird and the Edsel, which he describes as having a vaginal orifice. He is also distressed by the rubber breasts on the front bumpers of Cadillacs.

Like all autophobes, Mr. Keats talks about Detroit as though it is involved in a conspiracy to put over some outrageous scheme on an innocent American public. Yet while he attacks dat ole debil Detroit, he attacks the poor mortal who succumbs to the Devil, again in the hallowed Puritan manner. Here is how he describes Tom Wretch, a typical car buyer: "Tom is a member of that great middle majority that reaches from the upper-lower through the lower-middle class. In a word, he doesn't have much money and he's not too bright." Nothing infuriates Mr. Keats so much as the self-indulgence of buying a car on impulse. He sneers at the man who trades in a "car that works perfectly well at the moment. There is no good reason to turn it in. He does turn it in, however, lamely explaining that 'he just wanted a new one.'" One wonders if Mr. Keats would ache so openly to wring Tom

Wretch's neck if Tom would at least turn in his perfectly good but American-made car for a foreign one, however much he might have to go into debt. (But that's another thing that sets Mr. Keats and other puritans into a mad dance of disgust, installment buying.)

Here and there in a sudden whimsey Keats abandons puritanism, sobriety, the virtues of plain, paid-up, honest living, and appears as a devil-may-care Romantic. He concedes that our new superhighways have the virtues of being safer than the older roads, of allowing better gas economy, of opening up new countryside relatively free of billboards (autophobes, of course, hate billboards), and the like. Yet here is Mr. Keats' outburst of pique against even superhighways: "Yet the fact that the cluttered two-way highway is unsafe is solely responsible for the present transition to the sterile Autobahn, and so we may say that even the last vestige of adventure—physical danger—may disappear from American motoring as our Pablum stage of travel wears on." Instead of Pablum, Mr. Keats seems to want lumpy roughage. Not too many pages before, he castigated Detroit for not devoting itself to safety. Now he laments the disappearance of physical danger from American motoring.

Mr. Keats' catalogue of complaints, inconsistent and self-cancelling as it may be, does have the virtue of being exhaustive. It is perhaps excessive even in this, for he does not spare sports cars, exempt from the usual nonconformist indictment against automobiles. ("The sports car," he writes, "is specifically designed for the perpetual adolescent who feels a need to play at being a latter-day Barney Oldfield in an Ivy League beanie.") But he offers us compelling evidence on two points: the lengths to which an unflaggingly applied nonconformism can go in any particular area, and the pretty absolute incomprehension among nonconformists of the real place the automobile occupies in American life. Of course, the book is itself a most intriguing specimen testifying to the nearly pathological need of Americans to assuage a guilt over nothing less than being what they are.

We listen to Keats and his autophobic cohorts because we do have a puritanical streak. We may buy dishwashers, washing-machines, vacuum-cleaners, electric shavers, electric typewriters, air-conditioners, automatic sewing-machines, and the dozens of other mechanisms designed to make our lives softer, easier, simpler, even more luxurious, but there is nothing that says we must like doing so. In fact, there does seem to be something to say that we must not like all this: we'll buy all the gadgets and machines, but we'll also make it clear how decadent we think the whole business is. We'll engage in do-it-yourselfism no matter how much it may cost us.

The Consumer's Union *Reports* exemplify this schizoid approach very well. An article on power lawnmowers, say, will talk at length about the virtues of the "old-fashioned," muscle-propelled types and list the maimings and injuries and other catastrophes to be expected in using power-driven machines, and then very efficiently tabulate power models on the basis of how well they perform their horrendous jobs. The magazine will hem and haw about the need for freezers, pretty clearly intimating that anyone who buys one is not only likely to be self-indulgent, lazy, and inefficient but a spendthrift to boot; then it will tell you which are the best buys, and why. It will try to talk you out of buying a brand of a particular machine which costs more but is not necessarily "better," and make you feel vain for responding to its design or color or special luxury feature.

As a nation we do harbor a sickness of shame over all the vanities and sybaritic impulses Keats accuses us of, and I suppose we need books like his to purge us now and then. But the unsettling effect of nonconformist attacks on our habits and impulses is to make us accept a distorted view of our situation. We do indeed look on automobiles, highways, and traveling as abominations of one sort or another. We have neglected or demeaned the various satisfactions cars do bring. We tend to accept them as a necessary evil, classing them among the "curses of civilization."

No doubt the catalogue of horrors associated with automobiles—the huge annual death toll, the California smog, the havoc caused in education (high school students with cars do much poorer work as a group than those without cars), the temptations to overspend (with families ruining their health and stability as they overbuy), the unbalanced national dependence on the automobile industry, and so on and on—is genuine and formidable. I do not want in any way to minimize the social and economic dangers implicit in the present character of the automobile industry. But because these are so substantial as to be acknowledged by even the staunchest apologists for Detroit, we tend to overlook the very positive contributions the automobile has made to our way of life. We are so puritanically gloomy about cars that we concede too automatically that, yes, highways are monotonous, our destinations are not worth getting to, the scenery is blighted, the national parks are disgraced by peasants, cars are expensive and cumbersome, etc., etc.

Perhaps the most obvious fact about cars is the most neglected. The mass-produced automobile, as was recognized in the early days of the Ford assembly line, is a force for democracy. The social satirists like Huxley, lampooning our time with the phrase "in the year of our Ford," deplore democracy itself as much as they do mechanization. Anyone with a driver's license and the barest resources can own some sort of vehicle, from jalopy to juggernaut.

The horse once conferred mobility and security in the wide stretches of the American West. The car does the same now. The possibility of physically escaping an uncomfortable situation, of seeking greener and more hospitable land, of having one's vision and scope extended by the physical increase of an animal's power was recognized as so fundamentally necessary to a certain sort of life that horse stealing was punished by hanging. In a sense, the horse was inseparable from life. There were other factors, no doubt, requiring that horse thieves be dealt with so severely, but the import of the horse as a means of transport was basic.

Except within the largest cities, which happen to have their own means of public transit, cars today confer that mobility necessary to find and keep jobs. And in the California cities laid out on the basis of a network of freeways, the car is necessary inside the city as well. With cars we are not the slaves of our own physical limitations. Nor are we subject to the whims, discomforts, and expenses of public transportation.

The vast problems created by cars do not negate or even substantially diminish the benefits. Traffic, congestion, smog are inherent in the use of cars, in the existence of large cities in the first place, in the implications of civilization itself if you want to go back far enough. Like plumbing, sewage, water supply, gas and electric sources, the problems raised by cars are being solved, with maddening slowness perhaps. We are slaves of cars? No more than we are slaves of plumbing or electricity or any of the machines modern man is heir to. All of our measures for a better life entail responsibilities; even horses had to be fed and curried.

The car, then, with all its shortcomings and its sticky problems, confers independence. We may not use this independence as profitably, as wisely, as we might, but that is another issue, and has nothing to do with the nature of the car. More importantly, perhaps, the car, in conferring independence, inevitably confers another gift, the gift of a widened horizon. The automobile and the highway brought America closer in human terms. Country dwellers could visit the cities, and choose among the treasures cities offer: goods, recreation, and medical facilities. Los Angeles, Dallas, Kansas City have become cultural, medical, commercial centers for immense areas.

The car brought new vistas to all persons. Even the jaded city dweller, who perhaps needed least more varieties of human relations, who could do without the farmer and the cowboy, could still respond to countryside, to landscape, to panorama, to valley and mountain and plain and forest and ocean. If there is any validity in speaking of the broadening effects of travel, of reading, of going to museums, of attending concerts, then certainly some of these are to be found in our countryside as well, from the vantage point of our own cars. Visiting the Grand Canyon, Carlsbad Caverns, Yellowstone, touring the Southwest, offers edifications certainly different from those to be gained from visiting the great cathedrals and museums, but they are of the same order of experience, the order of discovering the nature of the universe. The most sophisticated student of painting and sculpture must find material to feast his eye and mind in the changing frame of the open landscape. Perhaps it is romantic to insist on the beneficent effects of landscape—there are persons after all who may hate to look at mountains and lakes and sky—but it is at least as valid a response as withdrawal into the sterile drawing room of finely drawn intellectual hatreds of everything various and multifarious in the wide world.

It is particularly unseemly to bring up the contribution of the automobile to our creature pleasures. This is one of the major grounds for our distress about cars. Yet clearly, if we relax just long enough to look at things as they are, not as we think they ought to be, we must concede that the automobile serves pre-eminently to fulfill our impulse for comforts that can come only with travel: vacations, short or extended, along the ocean; picnics in the mountains and woods; visits to distant friends and relatives and to cultural or merchandise centers; leisurely poking through the back roads; hunting and fishing excursions.

What about the infinite small pleasures and conveniences of the automobile? Do not these—convenience in local shopping, running errands, avoiding the elements, chances for sheer casual moving around, for occasional privacy—add up to an enriching benefit? Only the sourest, pruniest misanthrope would insist that we shop for junk anyway, it would do us good to be caught in the wind and the rain, we have nowhere important to go anyway, all we want privacy for is the dirty business of sex, and so on and on.

By itself, certainly, the car's function as a tool for casual and slight satisfactions is not significant, but it is an important additional reason for our dependence on it.

Only by denying to ourselves the right even to such simple pleasures can we make out a case that it is essentially corrupting, pernicious, to use cars so unproductively. The rest of the world, of course, does not use cars to the extent that Americans do, either for great or for slight causes, but this is not to say that it would not want to, or that it should not. Indeed, wherever the chance has offered itself, our civilized European friends have bought cars in huge numbers, creating traffic jams in Rome and Paris and London and Berlin. Even the ascetic Russians lust after cars as agonizingly as American teenagers, waiting patiently up to eight years to get one.

Cars are to be classed among the various liberating forces of modern life. That some of us misuse cars—just as we may misuse plumbing or television or electricity in general—is no reason at all for attacking them. To recognize shortcomings in the design and engineering of cars, to express uncertainty about the economic and sociological implications of the automobile industry, to worry about the hideous death toll of automobile accidents, should not be to lash out at automobiles and everything and everyone associated with them as though they were the scourge of our civilization. Undiscriminated, emotionally overcharged, uncritical polemics may serve some momentary neurotic need, but they do not enlighten us, they do not account in any way for the mysteries of social phenomena which we should indeed like to understand. They do not even improve any aspect of the situation: how seriously are we to take a plea for safer cars which is uttered in the same breath with a lament over the loss of "adventurous" danger on our improved highways?

We are as a nation excessively oriented around the automobile, but one wonders just how awful this really is. To the degree that owning an automobile signifies independence, to the degree that a car confers a certain freedom of the bonds of geography, to the degree that our society can direct itself to meeting the strong needs evidently rooted among our people to own cars, to that degree it would seem to me our automobile civilization may not be so heinous. We emphasize the sumptuary values perhaps too much as a general thing, and automobiles are but one of these. But I am not sure that we emphasize these to the exclusion of important human values, the values of health, of learning, of personal fulfillment.

Our values do after all rise from the people themselves and are not imposed by the outside forces of government or of nature or of overpopulation or terrain or setting. What people on earth would not want to be able to achieve the kind of life lived by most Americans? The desire for automobiles is by no means an exclusively American thing. We happen to have fulfilled this desire on so vast a scale, it sometimes looks as though the desire exists on this scale only in America.

But clearly the wish to have automobiles, like the wish to have any of the benefits of modern technology, from medicine through food to electrical household aids, is a universal one and connected with the deeper wishes to progress, to improve one's physical way through the world. Modern machines spare us sheer animal work. It is up to us to use the gifts machines bestow of energy, recreation, refreshment for more valuable purposes than sophomoric attacks on them.

SEVEN

I LIKE ADVERTISING

In his essay "Poetry and Advertising," S. I. Hayakawa, the semantics man, distinguishes between "venal poetry" —that is, advertising copy—and "disinterested poetry," which is simply the traditional poetry found in books, or scattered in magazines among the pages of advertising. Both kinds of poetry, he points out, "make every possible use of rhyme and rhythm, of words chosen for their connotative rather than their denotative values, of ambiguities that strike the level of unconscious responses as well as the conscious."

I am very pleased to have Mr. Hayakawa this far on my side, for I agree with him that "using our terms in this way, we see that our age is by no means deficient in poetry as is often charged. We have more access to poetry (or perhaps we should say poetry has more access to us) than has been the case at any other time in history."

Let me go a few steps beyond Mr. Hayakawa. I would add that we find in advertising not only poetry but some fine examples of modern art as well, and that in the design of the packages for many consumer goods we find some of the most interesting pieces of modern sculpture. I would like to be able to include advertising music in my catalogue of praise, simply for the sake of completeness, but except for the occasional catchy and trivial jingles, like the melody for Chiquita Banana's commercial about not putting bananas in the refrigerator, the only music worth noting in advertising has been either the heavily insistent and unsubtle things which sell items like cigarettes, or the affectedly symphonic fragments FM stations use to advertise some such object as espresso coffee or an exotic candy. I'm afraid I limit my own appreciation of advertising to the writing and the art work, and the combination of the two, not only in magazines and newspapers, but in animated form on television, which also adds the techniques of film montage, cinematography generally, including trick photography, cartoon animation, and even ballet. I would say, in sum, that our age has *more* access to *all* forms of art as a result of advertising.

When I say this, my nonconformist friends are quite sure I'm involved in a great ironic joke. How can anyone in his right mind these days with a straight face say a good word for commercials, for advertising which wants you actually to buy something you may have no wish to buy? Vance Packard's *The Hidden Persuaders* is a sustained, carefully documented exposé of the advertising industry's elaborate attempt to persuade us to buy things we had no idea we wanted or needed. Everyone, but everyone, knows how awful American culture is because of advertising. I suppose I could get nostalgic and bring up the phrases which spiced my childhood: "I'd Walk a Mile for a Camel," "Ask the Man Who Owns One," "There's a Ford in Your Future," "Children Cry for It," "His Master's Voice," "Time to Retire,"

"Often a Bridesmaid but Never a Bride." If nothing else, advertising slogans are part of folklore; they are richly evocative bits of Americana. The commercial of today is the memory of tomorrow. But who wants memories like this, my friends jeer.

I shrug. I know couples who adorn their walls with Scandinavian, French, Italian, and Spanish posters advertising everything from sardines to bullfights, who display foreign wine bottles in their windows, but who look at American equivalents with nothing but disdain. No doubt a bottle of Chianti has a handsome shape, and the label on it is exotic enough to look more like a design than a brand-name, but a Coca-Cola bottle and a bottle of Halo or Prell shampoo are also handsome objects—if we can manage to look only at the containers separated from the liquid insides and from the advertising. American posters advertising Renault Dauphines or Corvairs or the circus and some of our roadside billboards easily approach, sometimes equal, sometimes even surpass (!) European commercial art.

It really makes no difference in advertising whether fashionable people prefer European venal poetry rather than American. Advertising craftsmen, after all, unlike performers or writers, do not depend for success on fashion. Madison Avenue couldn't care less whether nonconformist insiders decorate their pads with bullfight posters or with advertisements for Fords or Camels. But it does make a difference, it seems to me, to our own sense of the outside world, to our own sense of how large the possibilities for expression and appreciation may be, if we exclude a tremendous area in which talented persons work. Hayakawa refers to "the increasing skill, talent, and ingenuity that are constantly being enlisted into advertising, publicity, and public relations as a result of the material rewards offered in those professions."

Now, really, what difference should it make in our response to the qualities of line, color, characterization in the posters of Toulouse-Lautrec whether or not these were made to advertise the Moulin Rouge night club? Are the qualities of art different in an abstract painting used in an ad for the Container Corporation of America from those in one that hangs on a museum wall? Are the lines of a single pot thrown on a wheel for museum display by "a native craftsman" inevitably superior to a jar mass-produced to carry mustard or jam in a supermarket? Are the technical aspects of ambiguity, alliteration, levels of meaning, imagination, economy of expression different for a slogan written to sell automobiles, "Better Buy Buick," or cigarettes, "Be Happy Go Lucky," than the lines written to seduce a young lady? Are the devices of expression in Marvell's "To His Coy Mistress" or Marlowe's "Come Live With Me and Be My Love" more or less seductive than the blandishments of a perfume ad or a brassiere ad?

In his contemptuous dismissal of American advertising, the nonconformist makes no exceptions on the basis of good or bad taste, truth or exaggeration, esthetic success or failure. He sweepingly casts out all advertising. Consider the campaign to ban advertising billboards from the new federally sponsored superhighways. The anti-billboard people say nothing about attractive or unattractive displays; their exclusion of advertising aims to be total. "I never saw a billboard lovely as a tree," their argument righteously proclaims. But it is simply another nonconformist groan against "commercialism," against another "symptom" of American conformism.

The billboard opponents generally say nothing about unattractive road bridges or lamp stanchions, the monotonous ugliness of endlessly flat and unadorned country. The highway system in and around New York City is determinedly free of billboards, allowing the driver an unobstructed, unrelieved view of black factory buildings, rows of squat frame and brick houses, marshes, metal scrap heaps, trash dumps, or heavy stone overpasses, which apparently constitute the standard of loveliness of Robert Moses.

Any cross-country driver knows the welcome break in the monotony of the turnpike of even the simplest sign: "Twenty Miles to Next Restaurant." Between the extremes of any billboards at all and none at all, there must surely be a happy medium which would control the content and form and number of billboards so as not to offend the sensitive driver, which will not detract from attractive countryside, which would even, in a positive way, delight and refresh any viewer, however mildly. I have for years found myself occasionally and fleetingly edified by the Burma Shave jingles.

The nonconformist may find deep satisfaction in staring at every cow chewing its cud and dropping its pile, in looking at millions of trees and acres of green, but I would gladly spare a cow, a tree, an acre, a hill, a lake now and then for a glimpse of a billboard with an attractive arrangement of line and color, perhaps even a pretty girl, and a message that is pithy, bright, ingenious, and a testimonial, however slight, to the creative gift of man.

The amenities of man do sometimes surpass the inanities and superfluities of nature. Certainly no poem of Kilmer's may ever have been as lovely as a tree, but I know of one or two works of Shakespeare, Donne, Keats,

Hopkins, Yeats, and Thomas that were. And I have seen such miserable, scrubby, depressing, stunted shrubs that I would have welcomed even the gaudiest billboard at that moment to rescue my sense of hope.

I do not want to make my case easy, as I think I might if I limited it to art work alone. It is easier to speak of the esthetic arrangement of lines, colors, forms in an advertisement in the same terms as we speak of them in a museum painting than it is to speak of advertising texts in the same way we do of poetry. Words, after all, do have meaning, and meaning has a content in addition to sound. While we may ignore the copy when looking at an advertisement as an artistic composition, considering the words as mere arrangements of lines, as they often are, we cannot do the same when considering the copy as language, separated from its typography. Yet it was Mr. Hayakawa who used the word "poetry" for advertising copy in the first place, and I accept it.

Nor do I think that the adjective "venal" very much vitiates labeling advertising copy as poetry. It is nothing new for poetry to be "available for hire," in spite of Mr. Hayakawa's approving quotation of Milton's contemptuous dismissal of the "trencher fury of the riming parasite." Milton's own pen was at the service of Cromwell, although one may argue that Milton was neither parasite nor prostitute; Milton's enlistment in the cause of the Commonwealth was a gesture of free dedication, not merely a means of livelihood. But Dryden and Shakespeare and Pope and Tennyson offer instances of poets using their skill, talent, and ingenuity in the cause, occasionally, at least, of "public relations." Queen Elizabeth had an army of respectable and talented men, "riming parasites" all, singing praises of her beauty, dubious though it was.

Surely, the fact that a poet may make his talent available for hire does not by itself constitute a basis for esthetic judgment. One may also argue that even "disinterested" poets often try to sell us something, and I am thinking not only of "party" poets like Dryden or Tennyson. Does not T. S. Eliot have a pitch at least as forthright as that of the unctuous elocutionist persuading us to buy a particular high-finned car? Do not Keats, Shelley, Yeats, Hopkins all have "messages" and do they not, one way or another, also persuade us? In the case of Yeats are we not convinced in spite of our skepticism of his "vision"?

Obviously, what distinguishes literature from advertising copy cannot simply be that one is "disinterested" and the other "venal." To distinguish between what is worthy to go into anthologies and what is worthy for the trash basket (even after a moment of pleasure) requires the application of criteria that are considerably more significant than the ones suggested by Mr. Hayakawa. I do not propose to consider here what the standards for literature may be except to say that they are flexible and objective enough to include at the lower end of their scale at least some of the writing which goes into advertising copy. Literature is a broad band and has never excluded the work of minor poets, the smaller gems of seventeenth-century lyric writers, even the limericks, humorous rhymes, light verse of Lear, Gilbert, Kipling, and Nash. We may even find in advertising the vigor of classical polemic, as in the famous text accompanying the declaration "A Hog Can Cross the Country Without Changing Trains—But YOU Can't!"

I quote below some gentler examples of advertising that should not be automatically offensive and might even offer to some a slight measure of delight. These simply happen to have struck my eye. I have also been pleased by the Edwardian tone of Brooks Brothers, J. Press, and Rolls Royce-Bentley advertisements, so neatly fitting style to product, and I have been bemused by the resemblance to seventeenth-century lyrics of the texts accompanying Warner's brassiere advertisements. On occasion I remember turning from the judicial prose of the *New York Times* with relief to the sprightlier, more carefully worked writing of the advertisements next to it (including the rather remarkably tasteful texts in that journal selling women's undergarments!). Perhaps someone ought to collect a fistful of literate or otherwise civilized advertisements in book form; an enterprising California producer has been running interesting animated television commercials as a full-length program.

. . . who's got the BUTTON?

A young man came into Wallachs last week and glanced around in a hesitant sort of way. When we asked if we could be of help, he said "I'd like to see a shirt or something . . . that is I thought I . . . perhaps I could buy a tie."

He picked up a tie, looked around cautiously and then confessed. He didn't want a tie. He was on his way to an appointment. A button had come off. He wondered if we . . . could it be possible . . . well, could we sew it on?

We could and we did. And if it ever happens to you, remember that you can always count on quick sartorial first-aid at *any* Wallachs store, any time. Happy to be of service.

plug that POCKET

A man made a purchase in Wallachs Fordham store, paid cash, put the change in his trousers pocket and the

quarters, dimes and pennies went rolling across the floor.
"Ought to get that hole fixed," he muttered. "Right away," replied the salesman. "Won't take a minute." And off they went to the tailor shop.

Now there are two kinds of holes that a man can have in his pocket. There is the above, the emergency variety. And there is the invisible or budgetary kind which is even worse.

In either case come to Wallachs. For the former we have a willing needle and thread. For the latter we offer the economy of quality clothes at reasonable prices and, if you wish, the added convenience of an Extended Charge Account. We may be old fashioned but we just hate to see anyone throw his money around.

those elusive STAYS

Many a man comes into Wallachs and quietly asks if we have any stays. Yes, stays.

Stays are those flat little doodads that tuck into those special "slots" on the underside of some shirt collars. Their function is to keep the points in position and wrinkle free.

They do a good job. The problem is how to keep them. Remembering to take them out when you send shirts to the laundry is next to impossible. And what the laundrymen do with them is a mystery. At any rate, they vanish.

We suggest one solution. If you ever need collar stays, stop in at Wallachs. We keep a supply on hand. No charge. Always happy to be of service.

Last Minute Bulletins on the Irish Geophysical Year

RE-SYNCHRONIZE YOUR WATCHES

Yes, we sincerely hope no Irish Whiskey research parties have pushed off for McMurdo yet. In the fever of launching the Irish Geophysical Year we (The Whiskey Distillers of Ireland) have utterly neglected two important aspects if one is to mount any sort of expedition at all.

A few minutes' delay now may save you much heartache later:
(1) EQUIPPING YOUR EXPEDITION. Shopping for provisions seems so simple and yet, at the hands of the novice, how complicated! Follow this simple rule of tongue: *Buy enough burnished, emphatic Irish Whiskey to go around. . . .* For other necessities such as ice picks and collapsible cups, you might enquire at Messrs. Abercrombie & Fitch or your local ironmonger's.
(2) PROVISIONS EN ROUTE. This is no great problem unless you fly. *Some airlines do not carry Irish Whiskey among their stores!* Before paying in your money send the form letter below. Although we do believe that were you to copy it out in a fair hand you might get a speedier, more thoughtful response. If you do not know the home address of the airline's president, send it to their local office; doubtless they will forward it to him. We are curious to know his answer so please drop us a line soon as you hear.

"We could be just as crowded at Macy's,
and not get wet!"

Brisk, exhilarating football weather is upon us once more and as thousands converge joyously on bowl and stadium. There may be some who shiver in their shoes, and wish they dared admit that they prefer steam heat to the great open spaces. We have a few suggestions for both the rugged and the frostbitten. As specialists in companionable crowds (which have made us what we are today—the World's Largest Store) we enjoy them, and delight in divining what they will want and need, and forthwith selling it to them, at low cash prices geared to make 94 cents act like a buck. That's why we are so well prepared at this moment to suggest that whether your corpuscles boldly respond to the challenge of rain, snow, and frost, or whether they'd rather just hang around where it's warm, we can make all Autumn expeditions pleasanter by fitting you out with appropriate woolies. So be your age, even though it's a mere thirty, and come to Macy's for warm socks, boots, underwear, sweaters, blankets, furs, coats, and ear muffs, before you set forth to exhilarate. We'll conserve your cash, as well as your body heat. As just another great popular American sport dependent on enthusiastic crowds, we are all in favor of football, but believe weather is something someone should do something about—and we've done it! For men, women, and small fry. So come to Macy's before you go to the game, and rub elbows with the smart and thrifty. Our low cash prices attract appreciative crowds. And crowds keep our prices low—a far from vicious circle in these taxing days when *everyone* feels the urge to save.

It's smart to be thrifty MACY'S

I have also been especially pleased by the text of the animated commercial on "Huckleberry Hound," a television half hour of cartoons for children. I quote only the words, excluding the whimsical action that accompanies them. (The action includes a scene of a dragon, snorting fire fiercely, burning himself by accident, licking his wound, then, as he realizes he is being watched, looking sheepishly at the camera, and, when he is described as "cross, ugly, impolite, you wouldn't like him," sticking out his tongue at the audience.)

ANNOUNCER: Once upon a time there was this dragon—cross, ugly . . . impolite . . . you wouldn't like him! *And* . . . there was this knight . . . trustworthyloyalhelpfulfriendlycourteouskindobedientcheerfulthriftybrave—altogether *different* from *dragons.* You'd hardly expect two so different fellows to get along very well. Well—

> meanwhile—back in Battle Creek Kellogg's was making Kellogg's Variety Pack. *You* know—ten personal portions of America's favorite cereals, like—Kellogg's Corn Flakes . . . and Rice Krispies . . . and Special K . . . and different kinds of cereals for—different kinds of folks. So, when this dragon and this knight . . . met ———*there* was Kellogg's Variety Pack, and there's where they got together. It takes all kinds of folks to make a world . . . But Kellogg's Variety Pack settles all differences. At least, different tastes at the breakfast table. Try it at your house.

At this point, I beg the reader to note carefully that, in the first place, I do not include *all* advertising copy in the realm of literature, and, in the second, I do not place *any* such work very high on the scale. What I do say is that some of the pleasures the cultivated man gets from reading the poems of Donne or Herrick or Marvell, or the cat poems of Eliot, or the (intentionally) lighter verse in the respectable weeklies and monthlies, are to be gotten, in much-attenuated form, to a slight degree, from some examples of advertising.

Mr. Hayakawa himself quotes Herrick's "When as in silks my Julia goes,/ Then, then, methinks, how sweetly flows/ The liquefaction of her clothes . . ." to indicate how difficult it is "to take delight in a woman's beauty without sounding like an advertisement." And just why shouldn't we delight in a woman's beauty *and* sound like an advertisement? Of course, if you answer that you cannot long delight in anything while continuing to sound like an advertisement, I shall entirely agree with you. But I shall also answer that no poem can delight if *it* sounds too much like other poems, nor are advertisers unaware of the diminishing effectiveness of the repetition of fresh expressions (they are not, obviously, unaware of the *increasing* effectiveness of mere nonsense repetition, which may or may not imply some obscure poetic principle connected with meter in itself). Note the gradual disuse of such striking formulations as "Be Happy Go Lucky," "I'd Walk a Mile for a Camel," "Ask the Man Who Owns One," "Better Buy Buick," "Man of Distinction," "Rheingold, the Dry Beer," "They Laughed When I Sat Down at the Piano."

I hope I do not have to concede in so many words that most advertising falls outside any realm of literature, that most copy is as outrageous as the verse of Edgar Guest or "Trees" by Joyce Kilmer, the art as puerile as most old-time *Saturday Evening Post* covers. No necessary relation exists between successful advertising and good writing; look through any collection of the classically "great" American advertisements, and you will find a museum of the mawkish, the foolish, the insipid, the smart-alecky, the cheaply clever, the dishonest. But this, I suppose, is to be expected from a medium that makes no pretense about appealing to as many people as possible.

Certainly more bad books, poems, pictures, musical compositions, pieces of sculpture, plays, movies have been produced during man's history than good ones. But even the worst examples of American advertising, if we can bring ourselves to consider them clinically, like so many repulsive specimens, may offer rewards in the degree of sociological truth which may emerge. Mr. Hayakawa remarks that both "venal" and "disinterested" poetry "have the common function of entering into our imaginations and shaping those idealizations of ourselves that determine, in large measure, our conduct." I still occasionally brood about what may be revealed of the

American need to prove oneself possessed of unexpected skills in the haunting advertisement declaring "They Laughed When I Sat Down at the Piano—But, When I Started to Play!" Or what the meaning may be of the open but apologetic prying into our sanitary habits in the hushed obscenity of the ads castigating "halitosis" and underarm odor. If nothing else may be gained from such speculation, it might be valuable to realize how brutally honest advertising copy can be about the most vulgar subjects in contrast to the pussyfooting of some of our most blatantly daring "disinterested" poets.

I also hope I do not have to repeat that I am not in any way concerned about the effectiveness in sales terms of any advertising. I do think Mr. Hayakawa overlooks a detail when he declares that the merit of the copywriter's poetry "is not measured by the pleasure it gives a single patron; it is measured by its influence on sales statistics." True enough, but the sales may well be affected by the pleasure the "venal" poetry gives to many patrons (just as a "disinterested" poet's work is accepted by an editor not because it may happen to please the editor alone, but because he expects that it will please the readers, that is, the several patrons of the magazine). But the question of sales has nothing to do with my point. There is no connection at all between an advertisement's compulsive effect on persons to buy and its merits as literary art. Many millions of persons, alas, remember affectionately the rhymes of Guest, Kilmer, Eugene Field, Riley, but we do not measure effectiveness of poetry in terms of statistics.

Mr. Hayakawa, I suppose it need hardly be said, had no intention whatsoever of saying anything complimentary about American advertising. Indeed, the only reason he made his point about "venal poetry" was in order to place the "blame" for "unpoetic" modern poetry, and to suggest that "disinterested" poetry might once again find its voice when American advertising found itself changing its tune. "All poetry," he declared, "has come to sound suspicious, so that disinterested poets are practically compelled not to sound poetic (as people ordinarily understand the term poetic) lest suggestions of venal purpose creep into their writing." This explanation of the forces affecting the idiom of modern poetry baffles me, for it leads to a merry-go-round. If "venal poetry" has taken its current idiom from the "disinterested poetry" of the past, will it not also take its future idiom from the new, "unpoetic," "disinterested" poetry of the present? And when "venal poetry" begins to sound like modern "disinterested" poetry, will this turn the "disinterested" poets back to the rhetoric of the past so that they will not *then* again be suspected of allowing "suggestions of venal purpose [to] creep into their writing"? Surely our contemporary poets do not "choose" their idiom in any such mechanical way. Poetic voice is determined by more important, more positive forces, than the mere fear of having its motives and origins suspected.

I think Mr. Hayakawa offers a more plausible explanation for the low state of "disinterested poetry," but he does not pursue it: "venal poetry," as he indicates, simply pays more. Even "disinterested poets," if they are interested in communicating with the public, seek out the markets that pay well; the best of today's "disinterested poetry" rather consistently appears in the magazines that pay the highest rates, or, at least, offer the best chance to establish a reputation, which itself is a form of payment.

Not all of the "venal poetry" in the pages of *The New Yorker* is superior to the "disinterested poetry," but some of it is, and the magazine's advertising pages are often as profitable to read as the text. (Of course, the best of that journal's "venal poetry" is far inferior to the best of the "disinterested" sort, but I would argue that both types fall within that broad band of literature I mentioned above, if at widely separated points.)

No doubt many "disinterested poets" spurn the sirens of Madison Avenue out of strength of character, preferring to use their considerable talent for their own private and unremunerative ends. But no doubt, too, there are at least some poets who are not sufficiently talented to make a free choice, or who may be "disinterested" only by virtue of being deaf to the sirens' song. It is these latter who, it would seem to me, create the apparent problem of modern poetry, which may well be, as Mr. Hayakawa intimates, a matter of developing an authentic tone. But the solution of any problem here, whatever it may be, is in the hands of the best of our "disinterested poets," and is not to be found in some hoped-for abandonment by American advertising magnates of their adaptation of poetry to their own ends.

I should like to turn Mr. Hayakawa's proposition around, and suggest that the health of "disinterested" poetry may well lie in its recognizing that, like advertising, it must find ways of communicating with the public without compromising its esthetic and moral values. Poetry has by its nature been an activity of those inclined to genuine nonconformity; the most effective poetic statement always demands a breaking away from the familiar, the ordinary, the conventional. Of course, poetry is also a way for a "man to speak to men," but the poet who stated this great truism was violating the principle of the previous age which held that poetry was the language of an aristocrat (of one sort or another) speaking to aristocrats. Poetry must constantly be re-examining its nature, its strategy for communication; it must periodically reconsider the nature of the speaker, the nature of the audience. In our own time, poetry has been beset principally, it would seem, by just this sort of question put in different ways: what is it, who speaks it, who hears it, to what end? Mr. Eliot suggested that "what we have to do is to bring poetry into the world in which the audience lives and to which it returns when it leaves the theatre."

Mr. Hayakawa's distinction between "venal" and "disinterested" poetry is a valid and very useful one, for it recognizes a true situation. But instead of concentrating, as he does, on the forces that make for opposition between the two forms, I would urge that we concentrate on the areas of identity. It is not likely that "venal" poetry will be much enhanced by such a study, for it has probably absorbed everything it can from "disinterested" poetry, with a grasping and unfeigned eagerness; but I should think that "disinterested" poetry might profitably go to school to "venal" poetry. "Venal" poetry has never lost the capacity to keep its audiences listening, often in spite of themselves.

I confess that my eye and ear are often more readily caught and held, and my mind stimulated, by the ads for the Hathaway shirt, Irish whiskeys, Qantas airlines, Barton's candy, than by the "disinterested" poem on the adjoining page, however noble my intention in opening the magazine in the first place. The "disinterested" poetry that will transport one for his own good, in a way that "venal" poetry would not dream of trying to do, must first catch and hold any reader.

John Crowe Ransom is one of America's eminent poets,

critics, and professors of English. Speaking before a Phi Beta Kappa audience in 1957, he quoted Whitman, "To have great poets, there must be great audiences, too." He had just wondered whether "we in the elite tradition of Phi Beta Kappa have held too hard and too long by our traditional literature, and have become culturally a little effete and devitalized." He concluded his address: "The barbarians who are our friends, the new people who write books, and prepare the programs for radio and television, these may now and then, I imagine, have more vitality and power than we like to allow. It is possible that what the arts need now is some tough but low-rated new strain in the stock which enters into the making of our artists."

EIGHT

WHAT'S WRONG WITH POPULAR CULTURE?

I LIKE American movies, jazz, television, radio (including soap operas and disc jockeys), popular songs, animated cartoons, Broadway and Hollywood musicals, baseball, football, several mass-circulation magazines, and even, as I have just argued, some commercials and advertisements. In short, I like much of popular culture, the things that millions of people are entertained by and respond to.

I say all this both defensively and aggressively because in certain circles you all but cut yourself off from civilization by making such a confession. Anything popular, anything which has a mass appeal, is considered as necessarily inferior and vulgar.

A professor I once knew announced proudly that he had never owned a radio, read a novel that was on the best-seller list, or seen an American cowboy or movie film. He claimed never to have heard of Cole Porter or Irving Berlin although he taught courses on the modern theater. He was proving his superiority of taste and judgment merely by announcing that he had never even bothered to taste and judge certain things. One drama critic declared that he would not go to see the Broadway production of Rodgers and Hammerstein's *Oklahoma!* because he knew how bad it would be just from the kind of thing it was advertised as being. Nonconformists, I am sure, applaud the professor's and the critic's position.

Some of our proudly nonconformist journals acknowledge the existence of movies and television only by running continuous snide criticsm of both. Radio, except for the stations playing classical music, most of them FM, has long ago been cast into outer darkness. *Life*, *Look*, *Time*, the *Saturday Evening Post*, the ladies' magazines are expected to produce an immediate shudder of revulsion when their names are brought up.

Every so often a popular-art type, or a personage with a huge mass following, is allowed entrance through a chink in the snob curtain and becomes an approved subject for highbrow and middlebrow discussion and approval. Examples are Charlie Chaplin; Cole Porter; some jazz combos and performers; the comic strips "Barnaby," "Peanuts," and "Pogo"; the late Fred Allen; Sid Caesar; some recent dimly lighted, tensely acted films (usually directed by Elia Kazan) and Alfred Hitchcock's early movies; and Hitchcock's television half-hours. "Punctuating [the darkness of television]," Leo Gurko writes in his book *Heroes, Highbrows and the Popular Mind*, "are one or two outstanding comedians like Sid Caesar and Groucho Marx."

But even with these the interest or pleasure is rarely intrinsic, is not in the thing itself, but in the way each of these reinforces one's nonconformist superiority. Fred Allen and Sid Caesar were admired more for their attacks on such horrors as vice presidents and old-time movies rather than for their merciless wit and parody alone, which were occasionally also directed against nonconformists and against French, Italian, and Japanese movies, so beloved by nonconformists. Chaplin, of course, has been apotheosized into one of the great critics of the contemporary social scene, which he undoubtedly was, but to the exclusion of his inspired slapstick; *Modern Times* is usually cited rather than the famous short in which a drunk is buffeted about by a house furnished like a museum gone mad. Nonconformists admire "Barnaby," "Peanuts," and "Pogo" for their social satire. Even the *High Noon* Westerns are interpreted as allegories of the individual opposed to society. And Hitchcock's recent nonconformist popularity depends much more on his television commercials, which rib the product and the sponsor (and are, apparently, marvelously effective as a selling technique), than on the half-hour plays he produces.

One might think that Cole Porter's ambiguous situation would suggest the inadequacy of indiscriminate, wholesale rejection of any popular form. His lyrics and melodies are sung in the movies and on radio and television, they sell records in the millions, yet they are admired by some pretty sophisticated highbrows (presumably on account of their cynical twists). If one popular song writer is acknowledged to turn out lyrics at least as good as those of the minor English poets of the seventeenth century, with whom Porter has been compared, why cannot another? Why not the late Hammerstein, or Berlin, or Loesser, or Lerner, or Mercer, or the late Hart? And, of course, they do turn out quite respectable verse (as do a number of others) as well as a good deal of garbage (although no more perhaps than you might find among the metaphysical poets or in the collected works of Wordsworth, Coleridge, or Tennyson). College anthologies will contain some pretty dubious stuff sometimes, both old and new, but rarely the work of a Tin Pan Alley lyricist. (Richard Wilbur, who wrote the lyrics for the Broadway musical adaptation of *Candide* is perhaps an exception, but then *Candide* itself was an exception: Leonard Bernstein wrote the music, and Lillian Hellman the book, both certified highbrows.)

The classical paradox, of course, is Shakespeare, whose work reached vast audiences during his day and since, and who is securely rooted in most highbrow pantheons. The occasional attempts to dismiss Shakespeare as crude, tasteless, excessive (from Pepys and others in the seventeenth century to Bernard Shaw and Wolcott Gibbs in our time) have been whimsical or half-hearted, and have, in any case, not seriously weakened his firm place. Equally futile have been efforts to claim Shakespeare for the elite alone, by arguing, for example, that Elizabethan theatergoers were actually superior to the general populace, and that the masses have never fully appreciated him anyway in spite of all evidence to the contrary. If anyone could be cited as proof that popular culture can have peaks that penetrate the empyrean of high culture, Shakespeare would seem to be an all but conclusive instance. But then discussions of taste with nonconformists are not expected to be cool, logical, or too fully based on testimony.

The problem, to put it generally first, is that there seems to be no available way for middlebrows and highbrows, even assuming their willingness, to respond to popular culture *on its own merits or shortcomings.* I squirm when I read a patronizing highbrow interpretation (such as Barzun's in his *God's Country and Mine*) of baseball as a mythical struggle among lovable natives, symbolizing something or other about the American Way of Life. Baseball is baseball, and while there may be larger, sociological explanations for its special popularity in the United States (and Japan), those explanations have nothing to do with why I or any other person enjoys watching the game. Middlebrows and highbrows need an excuse for liking a vastly popular sport. Or take Westerns. I wish some movie and television directors had never read analyses hinting that a wandering cowboy or a trail drive is somehow a reincarnation of Odysseus or the *Odyssey*, or a gun battle on a ranch the equivalent of the siege of Troy. Ignoring or condemning popular culture is a more honest way than anthropologizing it, making it something bigger and more mysterious than it is.

Which brings us to a more specific aspect of the problem. I am not saying that a work of popular art does not have overtones and implications and connections with a total and larger world outside it; all I am saying is that it is first of all itself. It must first of all be judged according to some serious esthetic standard, that is, a standard that will concern itself immediately and purely with the question of art. Obviously a work of high or low art is not worth discussing in any context at all if it does not exist first as a valid, authentic example of its form. Baseball is not worth talking about as a symbol of anything if it is not good baseball first.

We happen not to have much trouble with baseball, for most of the American population fancies itself, to one degree or another, as expert on that subject. (We do indeed have a remarkable, widely knowledgeable sense of the sport, ranging from the lore that accompanies the trading of baseball cards among boys to the literate critiques carried by *Sports Illustrated.*) The problem is in the vast landscape of popular entertainment, in which we respond instinctively, often without regard to expressed or sensed values, often in reaction only to the bludgeonings of determined persuasion campaigns.

The instances of Frank Sinatra and Elvis Presley illustrate the difficulty here. The success of both was in some measure due to their very carefully directed publicity. We can account for the success also on the basis of plausible sociological conjecture: both represented symbolic heroes to their fans: Sinatra, frail and superior to conventional melody, was a projection of youthful antagonism to a brawny and demandingly proper world; Presley, with his violently vulgar mannerisms, his simple and monotonous chant, is the next step in adolescent defiance and contempt for an ordered adult society. Yet however much publicity and sociology may account for the *mechanism* of popularity, they have very little to do with the merit of either singer.

If we go at the problem through these extrinsic devices, we put ourselves in a realm with no values but statistical ones. We cannot simply count records sold, millions earned, bobby-soxers enchanted. Sinatra and Presley would have to be all but equated on such standards. But I think it can be demonstrated, expertly and convincingly, that Sinatra happens to be a subtle, intelligent, highly accomplished artist in his craft, and that Presley is nothing of the sort. Now whatever one may feel about the talent of either, or about their success, the issue should be impersonal: are there standards for popular culture that may be applied in the world at large, not only by insiders, standards that are, like all serious esthetic criteria, objective, valid, and relevant?

I would say emphatically that there are, not only for popular singers, but for any performer or work in popular culture. Not only are such standards largely unformulated, however, but even the need for them is largely unrecognized. (It is often possible to use standards already available for high culture, like those for literature, but more often new standards must be developed, or old ones modified, as for popular singers.) The audiences for whom much popular culture is intended do not care much about esthetic standards, the basis of their response *is* undoubtedly instinctive and sociological, but the persons who condemn popular culture frequently do so without any qualms about values or rationality as well. Their condemnation is often as emotional and sociological (although from obviously different impulses) as is the acceptance of popular culture by the lowbrows they consider themselves superior to.

It is intriguing and exasperating that when some products of low culture are accepted by nonconformists, they are accepted with the same absence of discrimination with which other products are rejected. Foreign films are one example, of course, as though a poorly lighted Italian movie set in the slums cannot be as bad, and for the same reasons, as a brightly lit, American extravaganza in Technicolor set in a Southern mansion. After nonconformists put their seal of approval on detective novels, a similar lack of discrimination set in. I once heard a Columbia professor lump the all but illiterate Mickey Spillane with such careful and controlled workers as Dashiell Hammett and Raymond Chandler (although, to be sure, the heavily whimsical and intellectual Dorothy L. Sayers was considered superior to anyone else). Walt Disney's work has been acclaimed by nonconformists with all too little modulation, and with no separation of the wheat from the chaff. Most academic studies of popular culture (usually called "folk art") are blandly noncommittal as to the worth of the material they examine.

Of course when meaningful standards are applied to popular culture, there is no guarantee at all that a work or a form will be found to be worthy. Edmund Wilson, dean of American literary critics, focused his formidable attention on detective novels and concluded that they were, as a genre, inferior. Manny Farber's, James Agee's, Robert Warshow's movie reviews, which were published for years in middlebrow and highbrow journals and which went at their subject with an acute, solemn detachment, found many Hollywood products to be plain botches. But the point is that the conclusions here were derived from the application of objective, esthetic criteria and were not expressions of nonconformist prejudices.

Obviously, even after valid judgments are made, the question of individual taste always remains. It happens that I find myself bored now by detective novels, no matter who the author is (there was a time when I could not read enough of them); by comic strips, however much I may agree with the satiric sentiments expressed in any particular one, even when these are directed against nonconformists; and by TV variety shows, even when a comedian or a singer I like is on.

One of the things certainly wrong with popular culture is that the practitioners have so little meaningful, disinterested commentary to ruminate on. Whatever criticism is available comes from within the industry itself and can scarcely be considered selfless; often it has nothing to do with art, concerning itself with finance. Some Hollywood movie-makers ache to be helped, to be told honestly, in detail, where and how they have failed as artists. They take the rare serious criticism they get most earnestly. Otto Preminger, the director, engaged in an illuminating public exchange not long ago with Bosley Crowther, critic of the *New York Times*, who did not like one of Preminger's movies. Implicit in Preminger's challenge to Crowther, coloring the entire exchange, was a general plea for practical, creatively applicable analysis (for any movie) and not the frivolous, superior, easy formulations so many reviewers specialize in.

Every so often Hollywood signs up a perceptive critic such as Frank Nugent or James Agee, and sets him to work writing scripts. But the movies these days have attained almost the rank of a respectable art; there is even a quarterly devoted to film art, and low culture still has to go begging for a crust of hard-headed, uncompromisingly attentive, respectable, usable criticism. I once watched on television the unsavory spectacle of Al Capp, the creator of "Lil Abner," fending off the glib, hackneyed, indifferent attacks on his comic strip by a panel of smug nonconformist highbrows. In desperation, Mr. Capp resorted to citing the honorary degrees he had received for his work from enlightened universities. (Al Capp, incidentally, is another example of a craftsman in low culture who has been received cordially in the precincts of high. He has a substantial highbrow following, which obviously does not include the members of that panel, and was once the object of a respectful profile in *The New Yorker*.)

What is marvelously piquant about the whole subject is that a number of practitioners of high culture, the very darlings of the nonconformist bobby-soxers, would like nothing better than to gain applause on one of the many stages of low culture. Leonard Bernstein conducts the Philharmonic, writes symphonies, is a concert pianist—but also works very hard turning out Broadway musicals, including, hopefully, potential Hit Parade songs. Patrice Munsel, Dorothy Kirsten, Helen Traubel, Lawrence Tibbett, Ezio Pinza—Metropolitan Opera stars every one, were delighted to appear in night clubs, on Broadway, and in the movies. C. Day Lewis, advanced poet and critic of some stature, has written detective novels. Saul Steinberg, a modern artist with a unique style, draws animated television commercials. T. S. Eliot, the panjandrum of a large area of nonconformist high culture, has tried his hand at drawing-room comedy and at jazz rhythms in poetry.

The world of popular culture does happen to be an enormous panorama, and to wipe it out with an all-inclusive wave of the hand is to exile oneself from domains of all sorts and degrees of edifications and pleasures, pleasures which may even come to be approved one day on the rarefied hills of high culture. Also, to sample popular culture pretentiously is to lose the chance for spontaneous response, for evaluations which are original and private, however unfashionable.

Discovering the possibilities in the expanse of low culture can be a nearly traumatic experience, no doubt. It can have the unbalancing effect of an unknown natural wonder on an explorer. I once showed a professor, a specialist in the techniques of poetry, a song sheet containing currently popular lyrics. He had never seen such a thing and had never heard the songs it carried, and was overwhelmed. He congratulated me on making what seemed to him to be an archeological find. The sheets happened to be on sale at every newsstand. An important sociologist found himself one night with nothing to read but his children's comic books, which he had never noticed before; his next study contained extensive, excited, and extremely shrewd descriptions of the contents of comic books.

There is a tremendous amount of stuff in popular culture that is shoddy, abominable, worthless by any standards (except, perhaps, the most purely scientific and sociological). Much of this disappears more or less rapidly, and without a trace. If you try to recall some of the moronically repetitious rock-'n-roll numbers of just a few months ago, which were blared out by every jukebox and every radio, you can't; they have vanished. There is a large graveyard of weekly television shows that lasted exactly one season. Most movies are of the same sort. Some of the junk in popular culture perhaps never disappears, but we must always remember that it is only part of a much larger whole. High culture, too, has its quota of junk.

Perhaps more to be objected to than the obvious junk are some of the attempts to bridge low and high culture, to bring musical or literary or artistic classics to the "masses," or to bring "primitive" folk art to the "classes." The mélanges of Kostelanetz, Grofé, Melachrino, or Gould only corrupt taste; they have the mere surface of better things without the substances. Liberace's piano calisthenics, full of sound and fury, signify nothing. The music-verse mishmashes dedicated to such objects of affection as New York are not honest low culture and are hideous poetry and music. Television spectaculars of jam sessions are monstrosities of distortion: jazz is an intimate, an almost lonely art, to perform and to receive; it is miniaturistic, not elephantine. Much genuine simple folk music has been farcically ruined by being performed by huge ensembles of gowned choruses and formally dressed orchestras. Most annoying, to me at least, are the fiercely highbrow film epics, which achieve their "new highs in cinema art," to quote the advertising copy, only in the sensationalism of the dialogue, flamboyance of production, falsity of publicity, and the huge discrepancy between the expense and the achievement.

I have concentrated on popular entertainment, but popular culture in America, of course, manifests itself in many other places; in the design, for example, of furniture, household utensils, machines of various kinds. Wherever the creation or adaptation of vernacular objects, as they have been called, has been left to the unaffected, unguided instincts and talents of designers, engineers, businessmen, the results have been impressive, both in function and in form. John A. Kouwenhoven's extensive history of American vernacular design, *Made in America,* is an eloquent testimonial to the good taste inherent in at least this area of American popular culture. It is only when this natural good taste is overlaid with the veneer of snobbishness, which in our time takes the form of nonconformist sheer concern with how things should look, that we have to fear for the merit of the results: results like some of the affectedly "primitive" contemporary chairs, like the ice-cream-parlor chairs, which turn out to be neither comfortable nor especially durable, although they often are interesting exercises in wire and wood; or results like the faces of modern watches and clocks.

Low art and high art have in common a degree of authenticity, a satisfying of genuine needs of the persons who create it, of those who respond to it. Middle art is the consequence not of need but of expectation, of status-seeking, of yielding to needs quite external to the making or the receiving of the work. Middle art, I need hardly say, is the level of nonconformism. It requires no heart and no head to be apprehended; it requires only to be immediately apparent to the nonconformist populace at large as being like something else, something already fixed as "proper." For popular culture, the standard nonconformist manner is *conspicuous rejection*, the counterpart of that conspicuous consumption Thorstein Veblen found to be characteristic of the new rich.

All we have to do is have the courage to declare that the emperor is indeed wearing no clothes. Justice Oliver Wendell Holmes is supposed to have muttered while watching a burlesque house skit, "Thank God, I have low tastes." The return for our boldness in breaking the nonconformist mold might well be worth the risk, for our lives would not only be made less self-conscious and tense, as we relax and admit to all sorts of satisfactions, but the territories for pleasure, for enjoyment, on various levels, in varying degrees, would be so much more enlarged.

NINE

EDUCATIONIST, ANTI-EDUCATIONIST: A PLAGUE ON BOTH YOUR HOUSES

In the great debate on education that flared up when the Russians launched their satellites, scientists and engineers were among the leaders taking the extreme position in the attack on American schools. These critics lashed out fiercely, complaining that not enough science and mathematics were taught in the high schools, that students were illiterate, that teachers were incompetent, that the school year was too short, that there were too many frills on an equal par with solid courses, that Russia (and every European country for that matter) taught high school students much more, and so on and on.

While any dispassionate observer would surely find himself agreeing with many of the criticisms, he would also find himself, if he remained dispassionate, noting that many of the criticisms were clearly advanced from the top of the critics' heads, from the comfort of their armchairs, or on the basis of the most subjective and casual kind of examinations. As often as not, the criticisms were but remotely related to facts or to a larger context than the immediate and narrow one of the quality of the schools. Of course, the uncommitted observer was not likely to receive much help from the professional educators, some of whom, at the other extreme, defended themselves with the same emotional rhetoric and disregard for reality which their critics displayed in the attacks.

But it does seem possible to me to find a position between the two poles which is not only more temperate than either, but which happens to be in the area of a total reality. Certainly we must all agree that it is important to come to some practicable understanding regarding the nature and the future of American education.

Let me first consider Admiral Hyman Rickover's position. It represents the fiercest attack on American education and certainly embodies many of the points most of the critics have made. It seems to me also to contain some of the major weaknesses and fallacies of the attack. I will concentrate on his extended statement, "The World of the Uneducated," which he delivered as a speech, twice in one day, in Albuquerque, New Mexico—at a Rotarian luncheon and at an evening meeting at the University of New Mexico. It was also published, apparently with some slight changes, in *The Saturday Evening Post*. This document distills the essence of many of his other comments.

For one thing it is filled with generalizations that can apply to the Admiral's own position as well as to the enemy's. "The uneducated tend to overvalue their own abilities," he declares. "Never having experienced the travail of obtaining an education, they rarely understand how much one must know to handle intricate problems. . . . Even persons who are competent in a particular field, but otherwise deficient educationally, show the same tendency to overvalue their capacity and to interject themselves into areas where they lack competence."

Now, certainly, one of the most "intricate problems" in American civilization today is that of education, which involves, among other things, sociology, psychology, politics, history, finance, architecture, our whole system of values. Admiral Rickover's outstanding "competence" in his "particular field" (I am quoting the Admiral with no ironic intention but simply to show how easily his own words may apply to himself) does not necessarily make him competent to decide *ex cathedra*, as he often seems to do, on any of the thorny, messy issues of the American school system. Like any intelligent and concerned *layman* in the field of education, he has the right and the obligation to ask questions and not to settle for glib evasions, but I do not think that he himself is qualified to offer sweeping and conclusive answers. We all know how even the most noble cause can be harmed by some of its advocates. I occasionally feel that if Admiral Rickover is the sort of friend American education would have to depend on too heavily, it may need no enemies.

At one point, the Admiral implies that our school year of 180 days or so is too short. Now, length of the school year, as anyone knows who has ever considered the problem seriously *on the basis of experience*, is no way of guaranteeing that students will learn more. Putting students into classrooms with ignorant teachers and empty curricula for 360 days a year will only double their exposure to nothing; twice nothing is nothing. But there is even some doubt that doubling the school year with *good* teachers and *solid* curricula would necessarily double the learning. Some of the most famous universities in the world, Harvard, Oxford, Columbia, Cambridge, have very short sessions and require only a minimum of class attendance, or none at all.

"Any one who has ever tackled a difficult subject," the Admiral asserts, "such as higher mathematics, and used it to solve complicated problems, knows that he has emerged from his experience with a mind that functions better. Thereafter he will find it easier to tackle other subjects and other problems, because his mental capacity has grown." It happens that anyone who has taken elementary psychology is apt to be aware of the extensive experiments by Thorndike and Woodworth demonstrating that there is no such thing as "transfer of training" in formal disciplines, that the skills learned in studying mathematics or Latin or physics give no advantage in learning another subject. The findings of Thorndike have been repeatedly confirmed by the most skeptical investigators. The mind is simply not like the body, in which muscles cultivated for one sport may prove to be helpful in another. (Of course, sometimes they may be a hindrance.) It is possible to become adept in mathematics (particularly mathematics, which happens to a large extent to be a manipulatory rather than a judgment-requiring discipline) and remain inept, even stupid, in other areas. Witness the existence of "idiot savants" whose mental deficiency has not kept them from becoming mathematical wizards. (It is possible that the Admiral had in mind a less obvious principle than "transfer of training," but the other part of his statement, "his *mental capacity* has *grown*," is equally a product of superstition and popular misconception rather than any psychological truth.)

I am not saying that the Admiral is completely wrong

about either of the above statements. I, too, think that mathematics is indispensable to a full education, *but for its own sake*, for what it teaches of mathematical process and principle. I am saying that the Admiral's position happens not to be the only "educated" one.

A portion of the Admiral's statement declares that various humanistic areas must be covered to assure a genuine education. Of course, I could not agree with him more, but I am suspicious of just what he might mean by history, anthropology, philosophy, literature, music, art. If we look at the humanities courses required for graduation by our foremost engineering schools or by departments of science or by the military service academies, we see that often only the barest gesture is made toward including in the standard curriculum the various fields the Admiral mentions. Many engineering deans and technologically oriented physicists fight desperately to keep their students from "wasting" time in other than purely "useful" courses. In this regard, they happen to be much like Russian schools, which slight or distort literature, philosophy, history, psychology, economics, and similar disciplines. The Admiral's own oft-repeated charge that applicants for jobs in his office are "ignorant" is based on their poor technological training rather than on the narrowness of their education.

I find it uncomfortable to sustain an argument against Admiral Rickover, for he is obviously for virtue and against sin. He is stoutly for education and against ignorance. I join in his lament about the sad state of American education, but I am much troubled by some of his polemical tactics. It seems to me, for example, that he hurts his cause (and mine) by accusing "the uneducated" of possessing but one weapon in the discussion about education, "the lash of invective. They cannot argue on the level of facts and ideas, so they stoop to personal vilification." If the Admiral is right, and there is good evidence to support his charge, it seems to me that he does not aid his side by promptly adopting the same lash. (Some educationists, I should say, are more ready to examine "facts and ideas" than some anti-educationists.) Without ever identifying his opponents by name, he calls them bigoted, without "self-awareness," selfish, untruthful (could he possibly mean Conant, for example, who takes different positions from him on a number of critical issues?), and even illiterate (at the University of New Mexico meeting, the Admiral asked a hostile questioner whether the questioner could read). It would be very unfortunate, I think, if the Admiral's justifiably indignant and passionate rhetoric should obscure for any reasonable persons the force and logic of his position.

The Admiral rarely gets down to practical and concrete details in indicating what he thinks should be the content of education. We can only infer from his text what these details should be. For example, he quotes approvingly an "unknown sage" to the effect that "Great minds discuss ideas, average minds discuss events, small minds, people." One can only wonder whether Shakespeare and Dickens, Goethe and Dante, Tolstoy and Proust, are perhaps taught in a curriculum for small minds. It is true, one must sadly declare, that small minds, whatever they discuss, are always ready to reduce large and complex truths to easily digested, brightly plausible epigrams. I can only hope that this readiness is not what the Admiral believes a good education confers. (It happens also that one of the most popular ways for colleges of education to give their students a veneer of learning is to have them take a survey course in something like "Ideas of Western Man." The teaching of "ideas" is one of the most tempting ways to evade teaching substance.)

The professional educator can become just as heated as an admiral and propound the same sort of superficially persuasive proposition, which flatters one by seeming to appeal to the best instincts of logic and liberalism.

The fact is that the two opposing positions develop from the same narrow vision which is the result of a restricted, nonliberal, inhumane, "professionalized" schooling. I'll gladly accept the Admiral's word "training." Just because the Admiral seems occasionally to be describing no one else but himself does not make him wrong. The uneducated person is exactly what the Admiral says he is.

Following the Admiral's appearance at the University of New Mexico campus, I participated in a campus panel concerning colleges of education. My contribution to the discussion was a series of questions, which I thought ought to be answered by professional educators if the attacks launched by Admiral Rickover were to be convincingly countered or anticipated. One of these questions asked why colleges of education do not require their students to take foreign languages, mathematics, or genuine laboratory sciences. I was not answered, and afterward one of the professors of education on the panel insisted that my question was loaded against him. "Until you can prove," he said to me, "that home economics is not as rigorous a course as physics or chemistry, you cannot ask a fair question about our requirement in laboratory science."

It is extremely difficult to keep from being pushed farther into the opposite camp than one would like by the extravagances and inanities on either side. I read Rickover and my sympathies go out to the educationists; I hear the educationists, and I am convinced they deserve no better treatment than Rickover's.

Frankly, I despair of communicating with fanatics, of learning from them or persuading them. Their cleverness is often as strong as their conviction. In contending with them one indeed only risks being the victim of vilification and invective. In a way, society is fortunate that both sides take such extreme positions, for they cripple their own efforts by their incapacity or refusal to accommodate to reality. While the extremists will resist many of Conant's sanely considered recommendations on the American high school, it is likely that his report, the result of an examination of the actual situation in the high schools, will surely affect the nature of American education far more fundamentally than either the blasts of an admiral or the apologies of a professor of education.

The debate on education is profoundly affected by the social situation in which it is conducted. (The problem of education itself, no doubt, is a social one, but at the moment I am talking simply of the *discussion* of the problem.) It is exasperating that the opponents in the debate refuse to engage with one another. The arguments on either side are not answers or genuine challenges to the opposition but rhetorical exaggerations or distortions intended to sway an audience, or simply to prove one's orthodoxy. In effect we have no debate but rather an oratorical contest.

Perhaps the first step toward understanding the character of the contest is to recognize the degree to which an opinion on education promptly classifies one as being good or evil. It requires tremendous boldness to break through the complex of orthodoxies each side has built around itself to identify the faithful. A humanist (by which I mean in a loose and large way anyone who is somewhere on the same side of the fighting line as Admiral Rickover and who shares his objectives, if not his tactics or his weapons) risks his status as a humanist by suggesting, as I heard one bold and civilized chairman of a great department of English suggest, that basketball or football coaches may be as qualified to teach English as many English teachers.

An educationist who concedes that for many students their fourth year in high school is not only a waste of time but possibly a handicap for serious college work (as was indicated by a Ford Foundation project) may find himself read out of the profession. "The time is coming," the executive secretary of an affiliate of the National Education Association announced ominously to a state convention of elementary and high-school teachers, "when we may have to police our own ranks, weed out those who insist on being unprofessional."

If the atmosphere our professional teachers seem occasionally to want to foster in their organizations approaches that of a police state, in which the "professional" opinion on education will be nurtured by threats and intimidation, then it is only fair to compare the spirit of the anti-educationists to that of a lynch mob. I have attended public meetings at which every comment attacking education, however unfounded and wild, was applauded; every question seeking to elicit a fact or suggesting a less than damning answer regarding education was murmured down, or hissed down, or, at best, derisively laughed down. Loud was the cheering when Admiral Rickover rejected his questioner at the University of New Mexico with the retort: "Can you read?"

On education, then, as on so many nonconformist orthodoxies, one must be willing to have his intelligence, honesty, integrity, experience, disinterest challenged when he raises issues that have been resolved on the basis of gospel. Before I myself raise any specific questions, however, I want to bring up a larger one, essentially an *ad hominem* question, and challenge the characterizations offered of themselves by both the educationists and the anti-educationists.

The character of the educationist that he would like us to accept is that of the "democrat," concerned with "all" children, not merely those "gifted" to learn the traditional academic subjects; of the "tolerant, liberal, sensitive, responsive, non-authoritarian" person, the civilized man who knows the importance of emotion and character alongside that of thought, for whom every child is equally important, who has no hierarchy of snobbish values, who has been emancipated from unrealistic social distinctions; who is concerned with developing to his fullest potential the "whole" person; who wants to instill in every child all the graces necessary to a rich and satisfying life, commensurate, of course, always, with any individual's innate capacity.

In reality, the educationist is anything but "liberal" in allowing individual deviations among his students; he is anything but tolerant about departures from the decreed philosophies; he is snobbish and superior about his very nearly "revealed" religion, refusing to talk with unbelievers; he discriminates almost cruelly against a child of superior intellect, either labeling him as "gifted" and therefore rare and therefore creating problems in "democratic" teaching, or as "exceptional," lumping him with mentally deficient children, ignoring his genuine difference from some abstract little monster whom he has designated as "normal," and thus actually imposing an unnatural, ungraceful conformity on all children to approach this mediocre "average"; he is often so unlearned in the niceties of esthetic enterprises, art, music, poetry, that he is likely simply to encourage anarchic outbursts, without content, without self-fulfillment, when he thinks he is encouraging emotional expression; he is generally so unfamiliar with the humanities, philosophy, or history, that his thought and expression are likely to be hackneyed, littered with commonplaces, ungracefully embodied, often flagrantly ignorant of details educated persons take for granted.

I obviously cite the most benighted educationist, but to some degree even the most enlightened betrays similar shortcomings (a common one is indifference to the rules of statistics and logic) that make his noble protestations somewhat suspect. Of course, once adjustments are made for differences in vocabulary and perspective and experience and ideals, it is possible to communicate effectively and sometimes satisfyingly with enlightened educationists.

The typical anti-educationist, I regret to say (for my sentiments do fall into the anti-educationist camp), offers no less bleak a picture than that of the typical educationist. While he orates loudly (and often monotonously) on the subject of literacy, his own notions of literacy are often limited to such things as not splitting infinitives, not misusing "who" for "whom," and not using prepositions to end sentences with. He will say "between you and I" and will prefer the elegant, verbose, polysyllabic expression for the plain, short one. He will exalt the mechanical skill of spelling to a level equal with that of understanding poetry. While pretending to a respect for knowledge and learning, he will, without knowledge or learning, speak with definitive authority on our schools (and not simply as a citizen or as a parent). While paying seeming respect to the civilized virtues of modulation and qualification, he will see anything concerned with education in the starkest blacks and whites. He will leap to conclusions about anyone demurring from his tight orthodox position on education and offer appraisals of such a person's balance, sanity, ancestry, political affiliation, taste, instinct, intellectual capacity, etc. He will be as indifferent to statistics, facts, logic, reality as the most typical educationist. Yet the image the anti-educationist would like us to hold of him is of the enlightened, graceful, civilized, balanced, knowledgeable, selflessly dedicated gentleman, the product in his manner and in his substance of the best intentions of a classical education.

I think it important to establish that the opposing figures in the great dialogue on education are less than the ideals each imagines himself to be. Perhaps if their mere humanity is acknowledged, by themselves and by their allies, it will be possible to ask them a number of questions which are regularly evaded one way or another as being beneath their contempt.

To the educationist, then, I pose these questions: why are education students, by and large, among the intellectually poorest on a campus, showing up across the country with the lowest scores on such standardized examinations as the Graduate Record Examination? Do you really believe that a college graduate can consider himself educated without a meaningful exposure to a genuine laboratory science, mathematics beyond the high-school level, a foreign language? If you do, on what basis? If we consider their present education, can we fairly say that all elementary and high-school teachers are really underpaid? Why do so many high-school graduates come to college all but illiterate, unable to read or write on a level commensurate with their age and intelligence, often able, at best, only to perform meaningless exercises in sentence-parsing, punctuation, and spelling? Why is so much time in high school spent on nonintellectual, non-academic subjects? Is the last year in high school indeed a waste of the student's time? For that matter, might not the entire period of elementary and high school work be considerably shortened without any diminution in the quantity and quality of what the students learn? Is it necessary for "progressive" education to exclude from the school all of the classical disciplines?

The anti-educationist has many questions to answer also. Just whose fault is it, to begin with, that American schools are indeed so poor? Only the educationists'? Or does the entire social structure have something to do with it? Do students actually learn more when they go through traditionally taught courses in foreign languages, in which three years might be spent (as I myself happened to spend them) in learning the millions and millions of irregular verbs in French? Is it actually impossible for students following some of the techniques of contemporary education to learn anything? (My own son is learning more in the sixth grade in a school run by "educationists" than I ever did in that grade in a "traditional" school.) Just where may one find the bogeyman of progressive education in actual control of any school? Is it indeed possible that putting the emphasis on "basic" things (like the rules of grammar and spelling, the mechanics of arithmetical manipulation, the dates of wars) is an evasion of the true aims of education (genuine literacy, a firm grasp of mathematical principles, a cultivated sense of the complexity of history)? Isn't it possible to teach difficult subjects so that students *enjoy* learning them? Why cannot driver-training and typing, cooking and carpentry, be learned *in addition* to solid subjects? What is wrong with preparing our children to live in the small world of everyday affairs *as well as* in the larger civilization of the mind and the talents?

I do not really expect that either side will trouble to answer any of these questions, or any other questions for which they do not have ready formulations, simply because matters of detail, of fact, are actually irrelevant to the positions the educationists and anti-educationists take. Both sides are rooted in much larger social and historical movements, and it is these which determine the particular stands any individual educationist or anti-educationist may take, not relevant facts or philosophies in the context of the discussion.

The forces behind "progressive education" began, I suppose, with the French Revolution, although they may be seen possibly with more clarity in nineteenth-century England with the emergence of the new middle class. Education in western Europe since the Renaissance was an aristocratic prerogative; it was devoted, as it still is here and there, to "the making of gentlemen." Writers like Dickens reported the horrors and pointlessness of nineteenth-century English preparatory schools, but when it came time to send their own children to school, they sent them to just these institutions, to be stuffed with Greek, as Orwell put it. Nineteenth-century western education beyond the fundamentals was not only limited largely to the upper classes, it was also shallow, empty, mechanical, without relation to reality or to the actual humanistic values of the subject matter. One learned then, as he often does now, *in spite* of his schooling. (See George Orwell's comments on British public schools for example, in, "Such, Such Were the Joys.")

Dewey's philosophy of "progressive" education was, to put the matter very broadly, not only a reaction against the arbitrary, tyrannical, empty form of "traditional" education but actually an attempt to re-introduce meaning into education by relating the schooling to the children's wants and needs in a real world with a recognition of them as real persons. It was "democratic" and pragmatic in that it tried to detach the content and aims of schooling from fixed, class definitions and relate them to the creatures involved, regardless of the artificial expectations of social origin.

In detail, progressive education took many strange turns, at least partly because many of the practitioners were not as well educated as the founding philosophers. Certainly, the genuine sense of another language than one's own, of mathematics, of a physical science, of a social science, of literary values, of a philosophical idea, of moral meaning, of a historical trend—this sort of sense is intimately, indispensably related to becoming a full person in a full and very real society. It is the object of any free and large education to achieve such an end, but it is perhaps necessary to go through such an education, or something like it, to apprehend this fact intellectually and emotionally. Unfortunately, many of the persons professionally committed to advocating the glories of progressive education have little notion of what it means to be "traditionally" educated. Unfortunately, too, some persons mistakenly think they have been traditionally educated when they have only gone through the rigorous obstacle course of technological training.

One must make a similar indictment, it seems to me, of the anti-educationists, the proponents of "traditionalism." Of course, this is to be expected: the anti-educationists, most of them, were once the students of the educationists. They may differ with them but only in details; they would often substitute one sort of emptiness for another. Neither side understands, as far as I can make out, the philosophy involved in, for example, having an educational project rise out of the wishes of the students themselves (after the thoughtful but largely invisible direction of a wise, solidly educated teacher) and cutting across the traditional iron boundaries between disciplines.

Would not more be learned, for example, in studying the Greek language in connection with history, philosophy, literature, even science and mathematics, than through compartmentalizing each of these, studying grammar and vocabulary alone, dates and names out of context, multiplication tables and physical formulas in abstract, and so on and on? Obviously, skimming the material is as pointless and far less valuable even than mechanically memorizing much of it, but skimming and other forms of perverting the basic philosophy are common practice.

My sympathies are with the educationists here. It is pathetic to see devoted, intelligent men defending a philosophy whose roots and whose point they are often ignorant of or indifferent to. The product of an education which sedulously avoided coming to grips with any solid intellectual discipline, educationists cannot grasp the intrinsic value of such work, or the possibilities for functional application, the place of such discipline in fulfilling exactly the sort of objective implicit in Dewey's philosophy.

Upholding "democracy," the right of every individual to his fullest development, they betray this principle in any number of ways, most sadly by creating a hierarchy in which their own very good people must take a subordinate position to graduates of other colleges who have been exposed to and have assimilated the values of solid subjects. Instead of catering to the limits of capacity of their students, colleges of education cater to their limits of incapacity, their laziness, their indifference, their unwillingness to push themselves in "useless, impractical, functionless" disciplines, mathematics, science, language, etc. And, of course, because they cannot defend themselves philosophically or realistically, educationists do sometimes, at worst, behave just as Admiral Rickover described them as behaving; at best, they say nothing and owlishly pretend they have insight into a secret beyond mere peasants.

If I pity educationists, I am inclined often to despise their mindless opposition, which at least does not have the excuse of ignorance. I connect the outcry against American schools with the larger phenomenon of ritualistic liberalism and nonconformism in this country in recent years, the vulgar opposition to lynch spirit with lynch spirit. Anti-educationism for the orthodox nonconformist is simply another gesture defining his identity. He attacks American education in the same spirit as he attacks American mass culture in all of its details (Rickover sneers in passing at American advertising), as he dresses in certain fashions, as he pursues certain habits of buying, political preference, reading, entertainment, and of course, thinking.

The anti-educationist has only the remotest interest

in improving American education; it is necessary for his pose, his ceremony of rejection, for American education to appear in the worst light possible. He will not answer questions having to do with reality, for he may then have to look at the idol which he ceremonially vilifies with the eyes of truth instead of preconception. His identity as a member of a sect will become suspect if he does not mouth the appropriate mumbo-jumbo. In short, he will lose the security of being merged with a mob. He may extol individualism and independence, as part of his costume of nonconformism; he will fanatically praise the spirit of truth and free investigation and free thinking, as part of his pose as a liberal; but he will heap calumny, vilification, invective not only on any dyed-in-the-wool educationist but on anyone who dares to raise questions about the correctness of his orthodoxy.

Defining the nature of the controversy is only a preliminary step to dealing with the problem. Relating the present state of American education to history or philosophy or to the larger social situation in which it exists does not help us with the question of American education in the future.

American education, it must be obvious to anyone, educationist and anti-educationist included, is undergoing serious and meaningful scrutiny. Conant's work is only one example. But if the results of this examination are not to be sabotaged by vested interests and the irrelevant and irrational needs of the extremists, it seems to me we must acknowledge a number of fundamental principles.

Whether Russian education is more rigorous than ours or not, it is a fact that American education must in and of itself be improved. This would be true even if the Russian schools were far worse than ours. Whether we follow progressive or traditionalist principles, we must see to it that our teachers are more liberally and more intensively prepared for their work, that our students learn to range widely and probe deeply in meaningful subjects. (And I insist that we all know what "meaningful" means.) This is essential if we are to continue as a democracy, whether or not we face a threat from the outside. It seems to me to be committing suicide as a people if we cut ourselves off from the past, if we limit ourselves to the narrowest and shallowest enterprises we may be capable of as human beings instead of opening ourselves to the broadest, deepest, and most challenging.

We must not be content with letting any student do only what he may simply be comfortable with, regardless of his capacity; for his own sake as well as for the sake of society, each student should be encouraged, impelled, to go as far as he can, discomfort notwithstanding. When professional education fails to do this, when it takes the position that it does not matter if our young people are left uneducated or half-educated or improperly educated, it is violating its first duty to its charges, *on any sort of philosophy*, of implanting in our young the instinct and substance of what it is to be a human being.

TEN

OUR KNOW-NOTHING SCIENTISTS

WHEN I was a boy, one of my most frightening bogeymen was the scientist. I still remember my terror at seeing the Invisible Man pouring liquids from one test tube into another, drinking the mixture, becoming transparent, then launching on a spree of individual and mass murder, throttling policemen, derailing passenger trains. The Invisible Man and Mr. Hyde, who also drank brews that transformed one, took their place alongside Fu Manchu, snarling gang leaders, cowboy bad guys with black Stetsons, sadistic school teachers, Boris Karloff, Bela Lugosi, Lon Chaney. A white-coated, bespectacled man mixing liquids in a room filled with glass piping or standing before an instrument board with knobs and dials that controlled crackling giant electric sparks was a sure sign that something depraved would soon be taking place, like the manufacture of a death ray or a monster. It is no wonder that Frankenstein, the scientist, has always been confused in popular thought with the monster he created. Both the scientist and his product are equally terrifying.

It is of course anti-intellectual and lowbrow to continue in a fear of scientists (and their counterparts, the engineers) these days, especially since they have become celebrities like jazz musicians and baseball players. One television panel featured Norbert Wiener, the bearded cybernetics man from M.I.T., alongside Phil Rizzuto, clean-shaven ex-Yankee shortstop. And the scientist has even emerged from his obscure laboratory to participate in high councils of state. "I know many times we bowed out and did not answer the questions which were not technical and scientific," Dr. Oppenheimer was quoted as having remarked about his government experience. "Often we were seduced into answering them." And who but the lowest conformist would suggest that a scientist could not offer better advice on government problems than a mere politician or general?

In recent years, indeed, scientists have been giving the country the benefit of their wisdom on education (Teller), religion (Einstein), politics, military strategy (*Bulletin of the Atomic Scientists* is always running pieces on politics and military strategy). Of course, there is nothing wrong with any citizen expressing himself freely on any subject. But while most of us will not take seriously just anyone who has a theory about nuclear physics, some of us tend to listen reverently to the scientist or engineer, whether he talks on atoms, missiles, public schools, presidential candidates, churches, or our culture in general. My old fear of the scientists is returning as a result, for most technologists I have paid attention to are no more qualified to talk about any subject outside their very special field than most of us are about the inside of the atom.

The scientist indeed may be less qualified than the non-scientist to talk outside his field, for his education is likely to have been rigorously narrow. Unless he has had the good fortune to attend an old-fashioned liberal arts college, he will have had the most superficial and hurried contact with the social sciences and humanities. If he has gone to one of the larger colleges of engineering, many of which are now turning out scientists as well as engineers, his contact may well have been nonexistent, for many such schools design special humanities and social-science courses which have been dehydrated of their most vital content. He will not know the facts and concepts of history or sociology or the ideas and values of literature or philosophy. Even if the scientist's undergraduate studies were sufficiently humane and liberal, the world he moves in makes for narrowness and, except in his own discipline, for shallowness. A physical chemist, lamenting his restricted focus, once complained to me in desperation that he can scarcely keep up with the work being done in his particular specialty, let alone in physical chemistry itself; he long ago gave up hope of keeping up with the whole of chemistry. His only reading outside chemistry since his one undergraduate course in humanities was for an interdisciplinary honors class he was assigned to for one year.

Just what has brought about the transformation of the scientist from an evil figure in a remote, test-tube-cluttered laboratory to a contemporary culture hero at the center of our society? Certainly the publicity press releases attending the atom bomb had much to do with it, but long before Alamogordo and Hiroshima we were beginning to be impressed by the fabulous obscurity of the scientists. "Not even other scientists understand him," used to be the marveling comment about Einstein. Our society does respect learning and expertness, and the more recondite the learning and expertness are, the more they are respected. We simply have to be convinced of the genuine difficulty of the expertness, and the publicity—movies, books, magazine articles, newspaper features, television interviews—about our nuclear scientists has overwhelmingly persuaded us of the incredible complexity of their work.

As our scientists moved into areas that seemed quite mathematically pure—nuclear physics, for example—and out of the H. G. Wellsian or Aldous Huxleyan domains, in which they manipulated human life in one way or another, it became safe to respect scientists once again. We tend to approach our scientists with a fond protectiveness, and we are the more protective the more incomprehensible their findings. In a sense, we hesitate to offend or ignore them: who can afford to challenge the medicine man, the witch doctor? He may, after all, have magic on his side. Einstein had every word of his on politics and religion scrupulously, awesomely recorded, even when some of what he had to say was plain nonsense. We excuse our scientists from the normal rules of conduct; after all we cannot expect workers in ivory towers to behave like persons on the mundane plains below: all sorts of rationalizations, for example, were made to forgive the nuclear physicists for their loose and casual attitudes on security which were revealed during the atom spy investigations.

Some scientists, carried away by the public reverence of themselves, behave like culture heroes when they do appear in public, condescending, tolerant, graciously offering an oracular tidbit, a glimpse of their Olympian camaraderie. "He's a mean, caustic, and boorish man," Samuel Goudsmidt, co-formulator of the electron spin theory, remarked about an associate. "I once dined with him in a restaurant and he hounded the waiter until the poor fellow got so nervous he dropped his tray, and that made my friend howl with glee. To most people, he would be *persona non grata*. To me, he is a man who has solved difficult scientific problems, and in my home, he is welcome." The freemasonry of science would seem to justify any social behavior; it suggests the society of gods on Olympus, whimsically toying with men and feuding with each other, but also frequently aiding one another without regard to any other value but loyalty to the fraternity.

The peculiar and rare expertness of scientists has always compelled them to exist in enclaves—like circus performers, or movie actors, or Northwest loggers, or surgeons—where rules of morality and behavior and even of knowledge are much more familial and casual, and where one can safely and comfortably indulge oneself in lapses from ordinary requirements of deportment and evaluation. Scientists frequently present a front suggesting that they are devoted to more transcendent objectives than mere worldly ones (as when they resign from Los Alamos or from an aircraft company to join a university faculty to do "pure" research). With a sloganlike emphasis, some insist on the purity and remoteness from practicality of all of their research. This endows the research with the perfection of the abstract. It excludes questions of value or of guilt. It is a way also of removing themselves from the technological and manipulatory, the application of their work to the problems of actual human existence. Scientists pride themselves on being detached, unbiased, objective in their work, but, as Lionel Trilling has wondered, may not this very compulsion toward objectivity itself be a bias, itself be a way of avoiding an area of reality?

Even the hobbies of the scientists are arcane. Einstein

read Greek tragedy in the original; Oppenheimer knows Sanskrit; Goudsmidt studied Egyptology. Goudsmidt took up the study of scarabs when one of his college instructors complained that all he seemed interested in was the structure of the atom nucleus. The fact that Egyptian scarabs might be almost as obscure as protons and electrons seems not to have occurred to him.

One element in the scientist's current popularity may well be his youthfulness. A number of Nobelists in physics were in their early thirties when they received their awards. It seems to be an understanding among physicists that if a man has not made his great finding before he is thirty-five, he can consider himself washed up—at least in terms of being tapped for the Nobel Prize. A good number of the leading scientists and engineers at present engaged in nuclear and missiles research are in their thirties.

This youthfulness of the scientist, which puts him in the same endearing category with teen-age musical prodigies, chess players, and bonus baseball players, somewhat frightens me. I suspect, too, that, while the general public might be enchanted by the boy scientist, as by the child musician, and wish him well, there is a certain shakiness in the respect paid to him. After all, playing with hydrogen bombs or intercontinental ballistic missiles is not quite the same as playing with a bat and ball or a piano or a chess set. Mixed with the public respect for the boy scientist is an apprehensive hope that he really knows what he is doing.

But what kind of a discipline must the study of physics be if it can be mastered and revolutionized by a man before he is thirty? It must be of the very special order which includes the playing of chess, of musical instruments, and of sports. No doubt great talent or genius is essential to becoming outstanding in any of these fields. The admiration and respect of the ordinary man naturally go out to chess champions, musical performers, home-run hitters, as they do to acrobats, animal trainers, great inventors, ingenious wood-whittlers, and all sorts of persons with unique skills. Without meaning in any way to obscure or denigrate the special nature of scientific study, I submit that any area in which a man can make his greatest achievement so early in his life is not one in which the special capacities that come with maturity—wisdom, ripeness, extensive as well as intensive knowledge, balance, subtlety, breadth of vision, a developed moral sense, a system of values, etc.—are normally employed.

Now I am perfectly happy, delighted, that our country has been able to turn out brilliant young scientists. But my happiness does not prevent me from asking certain questions: how much history do these young men know, how much literature, how much social science, how much philosophy, how are they different from their youthful counterparts in the Soviet Union, or under Nazi Germany? Are they like the British scientists who defected to Russia? Might they ever become like the Nazi engineers and scientists who perverted science to the ends of barbarism? I do not much care whether the boy who leaves high school to pitch for the Milwaukee Braves knows his history or not; or whether Van Cliburn happened to have read Arthur Koestler or George Orwell before he made his trip to Moscow; but I do care whether the chief scientist at one of our rocket-testing stations has a sense of the relation of his work to human history, to human capacity, to human values. Does he really know the difference between an electronic brain and a human one?

The professional and personal alienation from society

of the scientist is trivial compared with his political innocence. His naïveté in politics can lead to disaster. The casualness of some atomic scientists toward security before Russia perfected her atom bomb was no doubt a reasoned thing, based on the certainty that Russia would inevitably have the bomb simply by following widely known principles. But for some scientists, at least, the casualness was the result of a simple-mindedness about Communism. Goudsmidt was ready in the midst of the war, while engaged on an American mission connected with the atom bomb, to rush off for a *gemütlich* reunion in Switzerland with an old friend and teacher, Werner Heisenberg, the Nazi counterpart of Oppenheimer. He hoped, he explained to the military man assigned to accompany him, that in the course of the surely warm and excited conversation, he would pick up some scraps to indicate the extent of German exploration of the atom. "And while he's giving you a lead on them, why wouldn't you be giving him a lead on us?" his dry, practical colleague wanted to know, forbidding the rendezvous.

A liberal education hopefully gives a man a meaningful and fixed area from which to view the world, in which to root his values, from which to recognize the complexity and often indeterminate nature of moral and political problems. It does not encourage a whimsical shifting of ground. In the course of a book-length account of Edward Teller's "paternity" of the H-bomb, he is described, at one time, as languishing on the A-bomb (intended for Germany and Japan), then vigorously supporting the development of the H-bomb (during the early days of the cold war with Russia), and, at still another time, disclaiming the need of scientists to be impelled by political considerations at all in offering their advice or their skills. It will be remembered that the decision to develop the H-bomb was in large measure based on political and philosophical considerations, many of these settled by politicians and statesmen. Whether the decision was good or bad is not to the point at present; what is to the point is that no pure scientist using only his pure science could have contributed very much to the ultimate decision.

Von Braun's case is more illuminating. He may be no more responsible, as he claims, for the V-2's being launched against London than Einstein was for the atom bomb. (The parallel eludes me: Einstein's formula, $e = mc^2$, was abstract and had nothing to do with Hiroshima, which was many years away; Von Braun worked not on a principle of physics but on a weapon whose specific function was to kill civilians in London. And even if Einstein had been as active as Von Braun in the development of hardware, there surely was a basic moral difference between helping the Nazis to beat the Allies, and vice versa.) Von Braun takes himself, to judge from the portrait of him in Daniel Lang's book, *The Man in the Thick Lead Suit*, as another figure in the great tradition of dedicated scientists, committed entirely to the pursuit of knowledge, wherever it may take him. Yet we are expected to sympathize with him when we read the record of how the stupid, vulgar, ignorant, boorish Nazi bureaucrats prevented him from concentrating fully on his scientific work—which aimed, ultimately, at the perfection of a revenge rocket to hit New York! The book, *V-2*, by Von Braun's superior at Peenemünde (the German rocket-testing station), General Walter Dornberger, sustains this particular and astonishing complaint throughout its length, that Hitler interfered with the perfection of the vengeance rocket against civilians, making as its sole gesture toward decency a reference, in the preface, to the peacetime possibilities of rockets.

Goudsmidt's report of his mission with the invasion forces to determine the state of German atomic development provides additional evidence of the moral emptiness of German science. "If only the government had taken the true scientists into its confidence instead of . . . charlatans," the Germans complained to Goudsmidt. Most competent German scientists became anti-Nazi only after they were insultingly rejected by the Nazis. Goudsmidt analyzes Heisenberg's opposition to the Nazis as follows:

> "Although he fought courageously against Nazi excesses and especially Nazi stupidities, his motives were not as noble as one might have hoped from such a great man. He fought the Nazis not because they were bad, but because they were bad for Germany, or at least for German science. His principal concern was that Germany might lose its lead in science, especially physics. That is why he strenuously objected to the exile of German Jewish physicists."

Goudsmidt records the macabre and meaningless thoroughness of the German scientific mind. He described the graphs that were kept of the temperature rise of a man who was frozen nearly to death, then subjected to "rewarming by one woman," "rewarming by two women," and "rewarming by women after coitus."

Goudsmidt quite clearly sees that the ugly failure of German science was not a matter of individual frailty. "It was indeed a serious indictment of the German system of education that it produced men who could, at one time, have done outstanding work in a narrow field of research, and yet proved themselves to be dangerously unbalanced in their judgment and behavior once outside their specialized rut. Such men can hardly be called scholars, or even educated human beings. They have the characteristics of a machine or a super robot, which performs a certain prescribed task absolutely correctly, but blows the fuse if used for some task other than that for which it was built."

One is tempted strongly to forgive the sentiments of persons conditioned by Nazis. Von Braun has now spent more than a decade in the United States. He has even expressed himself as having come to believe that religion is man's answer to his problems of politics. On a recent trip to London, however, Von Braun was asked what he thought of his vengeance rockets that fell on the city. According to the newspapers, he defended himself vigorously and declared, among other things, "My country right or wrong."

Von Braun's philosophy, his orientation in the world, may have less to do with his being brought up under Hitler than with his simply being brought up in the world of science. Mrs. Enrico Fermi, for example, who happens to be Jewish like Goudsmidt, mentions in her amiable reminiscences the nuisance of her Jewishness with a wry hesitancy as being perhaps the chief reason why the Fermis left Italy when Mussolini introduced an Italian version of the Nuremberg laws. Fascism itself, to judge from her record, scarcely bothered the Fermis in its other ideological aspects.

I am glad that Von Braun is on our side rather than on the Russians', and that Fermi came to the United States and did not remain in Italy. But I must wonder, perhaps cynically, how much difference it would have made to Von Braun if the Russians had got to him first, as they did to many of his colleagues, and whether, if Mussolini had not adopted anti-Semitism, the Fermis would really have come to America.

I emphasize that I am frightened by the scientific spirit, not because it could develop intercontinental ballistic missiles, but because it could fret when the high command interfered with allowing the development of a missile to fall on New York. I am not frightened by the spirit which prompts the physician to heal all men, but by the one that prompted the German doctors to experiment on human beings; not by the spirit that will devote itself to increasing food production, but by the one that will turn up a theory, the way Lysenko did, to satisfy ideological needs.

In short, I am not frightened by the objectivity, detachment, respect for truth, selflessness, dedication to method, which we are told over and over again are the marks of the scientist; these I admire and respect and am in awe of. But I am frightened when these characteristics are not grounded in a respect for human history and human value, when these are free-floating, for sale to any bidder who happens to be around, when these characteristics are perverted, in the very name of science, to the services of the depraved and immoral or inhuman; I am terrified when these characteristics are exalted by the scientists themselves or by their sophomoric admirers into supreme values that take precedence over all other values.

I intend no facile paradox when I describe our scientists as "know-nothing." Their knowledge of physics and chemistry and chess and hi-fi and engineering and mathematics, even of Sanskrit and Greek (I am not sure about Egyptology), are attainments not very far superior to the skills of electronic machines. To be sure, machines cannot make complex judgments; they cannot make moral evaluations; they cannot use history and literature; they cannot respond esthetically. But to what serious extent can scientists as a class do these things respectably? There are without question many, many individual scientists as humane and as politically sophisticated as any man of good education, but when they are so they have broken the barriers of their institutional education. Physicians, too, biological as well as physical scientists, and engineers are also likely to be bigoted and illiterate as a direct result of their particular education.

It is no counter argument at all to point to persons in the humanities as also deserving the designation of "know nothing." I am uncomfortably aware of many academic persons in English, languages, history, social science, philosophy; of writers and painters and musicians, who are dense and intolerant about world and national politics, science, history, business, philosophy, popular culture—in short, the full and varied world of mankind. This is no less tragic than the scientists' lack of scope and depth. But at least we cannot blame their education: their ignorance is personal and willful and not the result of social and institutional forces. They have been exposed at some length to the proper influences. It is not, so to speak, inevitable under the circumstances. Nor is it as likely to be fraught with danger. Humanists, enlightened or otherwise, will not be the ones who, like the two military scientists in E. B. White's short story, will be circling the earth in a satellite, able to press the button of Armageddon. Persons in the humanities will never have buttons to press, for better or worse; they are simply not in the business of counting backwards from ten.

Recently, a brilliant young colleague of mine, a mammalogist, and I spent an evening arguing the opposition between the scientist and the humanist. This was the climax of a series of skirmishes that had extended over several years. I was very pleased to engage with him, for, unlike most scientists, he was aware of the conflict and willing to argue the matter, to teach or be taught. Many scientists and engineers are scarcely conscious that there is another view of the universe than their own mechanistic one. Some who are so aware will not deign to enlighten the ignorant, fuzzy-headed humanist; they will not stoop to discussion or argument.

My friend and I joined the issue rather promptly on the subject of sex, with specific reference to Kinsey's work and to Lionel Trilling's critique of the Report in his book *The Liberal Imagination*. We were at loggerheads at once. I defined sex as having to do with relations between human beings; he as having to do with evolution. I think I put it fairly when I say that I, having read Darwin, understood what he meant; but he, not having read, say, Shakespeare or Lawrence or Meredith or the Brontës, insisted that my definition was quite meaningless. He insisted that one could find out nothing useful about the subject from studying novelists, that Kinsey's method, whatever shortcomings there may have been in details, was the only way of ascertaining the nature of any sort of truth.

However much one can discover about the world by pursuing the best scientific method, one can obviously not discover everything. I submit that there is at least an area as large as that staked out by science which can be explored only by the humanist, by the person who, first by education, then perhaps by temperament, knows the world through his senses, instincts, experiences, tastes, intuitions, emotions; all of these appropriately cultivated, appropriately apprehended, appropriately applied. The scientist is usually barred from this area, for he has not only not been introduced to specific portions of it, he has been totally discouraged from acknowledging the possibility that it exists, or, if it does exist, that it has any validity. Whatever latent tendencies he may have had to trust his subjective responses have either been allowed to atrophy for lack of nourishment or have been deliberately destroyed by the constant poison fed into his intellectual system by his training.

My friend was not denying the existence and power of nonscientific forces, the values of emotional and esthetic response, the creativity of imagination and thought; he was denying, as I understood him, their usefulness in determining the nature of man and of the world. The humanist's values, he said, are much too personal, impressionistic, and arbitrary, often a mere matter of taste; they shift constantly, from person to person, place to place, time to time; they are imprecise, ephemeral, without limits or substance. Of course, he is right, and he was accurately describing the nature of man.

The way of the humanist—if I may use the term to include the painter, the musician, the writer, the philosopher—is to use himself, his senses, his mind, his particularly developed artfulness, not only to explore the world, to uncover recognizable but hitherto unapprehended territories, but, far more importantly perhaps, *to make new things*. The humanist's way of recording and creating is certainly not the scientist's. But only through an evil and grotesque distortion of the nature of man, of the sort that is imagined in *Brave New World* and in *1984*, will the scientist ever imagine himself as capable of separating every last component that goes into emotional vitality or creative attainment, and feed these into machines. Only in a society where persons have lost their humanity will machines stimulate sexual awareness or turn out novels.

sonnet, looking at a painting, listening to a sonata. The tactics and strategy of science, its products, its details of fact and procedure are as liberalizing as the substance of literature and history and philosophy. Even the products of engineering belong to the heart of the humanities: consider bridges and roads and buildings; plants for cracking oils or for producing electricity; dams, automobiles, the dozens of daily things we use. Many critics have justly placed engineered objects alongside more purely created ones, nonfunctional ones, and have been as much enchanted with the operation of the things as with their appearance. The range of the humanities would be unwholesomely constricted if they were ever thought to exclude science, mathematics, or technology.

It would be easy, I think, to make out a utilitarian argument for scientists, engineers, technologists to study the humanities. Such arguments are repeatedly made out for businessmen. The humanities will help you get ahead; you will know what to talk about; you will have interests to occupy your leisure time; you will make better objects; you will make more money; you will understand better what you are doing. Yet the best argument, it seems to me, has nothing to do with usefulness or value in any sense of application to design, business, research, or after-work living. The best argument for knowing something rather than knowing nothing must be one that does not root itself in the practical at all. The best argument for knowledge must ultimately be based on the realization that knowledge is "useless" in many of the ways we sometimes say it may be used.

The liberal arts, a liberal education, the humanities, if we pause to consider the implication of the words themselves, are designed to make us "free" as "human beings."

The more we know about everything and anything, the more we realize how little we know, the more fulfilled we become as human beings, the more ready we are to learn, to grow, to extend the areas of our knowledge.

Precisely because my friend the mammalogist asks questions, is aware of the issue, does not take it as settled, doubts himself and doubts me, he is in the best sense a humanist liberally trained. The fact that he has a tremendous faith in science in no whit detracts from his liberalism or humanism. Scientists who understand and appreciate the humanities are never lesser scientists: they are better ones.

Scientists like Oppenheimer, who seem aware of the limits of their wisdom, do not trouble me. I am afraid of our know-nothing scientists precisely because this group does not seem to know how little it knows. One of the signs of an ignorant man, of course, in all ages has been his incapacity to realize how ignorant he is. To the degree that scientists positively know how much they know, to that degree I fear them. I do not trust the invisible scientist—or Frankenstein, or the practitioners of prefrontal lobotomy, or engineers who forget that bridges and machines are ultimately for people—to make decisions involving mankind, or myself personally, or to attain a place in our society of oracles and elder statesmen. Until their education will ensure their knowing something—most of all the limits of their knowledge—the scientist in our society does indeed bear being feared and watched.

ELEVEN

CAN COLLEGE TEACHERS TEACH?

IN CONCENTRATING on the problems of elementary and high-school education, we often neglect the far greater problems of college education. It is in college, after all, where we prepare our scientists, teachers, doctors, lawyers, engineers, military leaders. The colleges are filling up, slowly and steadily, to the bursting point. In part, the increase in college enrollment is the result of the increased birth rate in the country, but in considerable measure, too, it is the result of an increased demand for a college education. Not only is the absolute number of college students increasing, but so is the proportion of young people graduating from high school who want a college degree. It is inevitable that the various current pressures on the colleges will profoundly affect the nature of higher education in the next decade or so.

The complaints have already started to be filed. One of the most common is that we are allowing too many inadequately prepared students to register in college. These waste valuable space and time and adulterate the quality of the courses they take as long as they remain in college, which often is not terribly long. Another complaint has to do with the quality of college instruction. Writing in *Parade*, a nationally distributed Sunday supplement, Dr. Earl J. McGrath, a former U. S. Commissioner of Education, indicated that what was wrong with college teaching is that the professors often do not know how to teach, that they lack training in professional education courses, that the content they know of a particular subject matter often has little to do with what they have to teach undergraduates. These two complaints seem to me closely intertwined and they may hit at what seems to me the fundamental question in higher education: can college teachers teach? All other issues, one way or another, are subordinate to the critical one of what and how much is learned in college.

There is little question that large numbers of high-school students are poorly prepared to do college work in English, mathematics, laboratory science, languages, the social sciences. They often cannot read or write beyond the most primitive level; they do not know fundamental operations in arithmetic, let alone the fundamentals of geometry, algebra, or trigonometry; they have little or no acquaintance with history, the details of government, world affairs. In short, they have been very poorly prepared for doing college work of the traditional sort. Admiral Rickover is quite right in lamenting the shallowness and ignorance of so many of our high-school graduates.

But the two most commonly offered solutions for improving the quality of high-school graduates simply complicate the problem. If colleges raise entrance requirements, as is advocated by many critics of the high schools, the colleges involve themselves in a paradox: they berate the high schools for the poor teaching and then punish high-school graduates for not knowing enough to enter college. Obviously, if the high schools do not, indeed, teach enough, then their students will not know enough. It is manifestly unfair to penalize a student for a situation which he did not make. The least the colleges might do, if their complaints about high-school teaching have any validity, is to give the graduates the chance to show how they might perform, how much they might learn in college, under expert, hard-headed, uncompromising instruction. Any number of potentially able students do not find themselves until sometime during their first year of college; these would be lost if we exercised excessively strict screening devices. It is possible that if colleges absolutely refused to accept unprepared students, public pressure would eventually compel the high schools to improve their teaching. This seems already to be happening to some extent. But it is doubtful for a number of reasons that the high schools could do very much more than they are doing now; I discuss one of these reasons below, the education of high-school teachers. Also, some students will never do their best in high school under any circumstances, but will show up well in college.

In addition, it is especially unjust for colleges to criticize high-school teaching without acknowledging their responsibility for the high-school teachers. If high-school teachers do indeed concentrate in their preparation on the methods of teaching, rather than on the content of their subjects, it would seem to be no one's fault but the colleges'. This, of course, may be only the fault and responsibility of the schools of education, which set up the course requirements for their students. But there is an inclination in subject-matter departments—sciences, social sciences, humanities—to evaluate education students much more gently than others. Where other students would be failed for poor work in English, say, an education student is likely to be passed on the ground that, after all, he will not be working as a writer or scholar or critic, he will "only" be teaching English to high-school students.

Of course, at this point the educationist will charge that colleges do not bother to teach their students the sort of subject matter they will have to teach in the high school classroom. I heard the administrator of high-school science programs in Albuquerque, a nationally known figure, Dr. Eldred R. Harrington, suggest that future teachers of high-school mathematics would do better to take a lot of work in "lower" mathematics, which they would be teaching in their classes, rather than any work in higher mathematics, like calculus, which they would never have to teach in high school. He expressed himself as dubious about the value of calculus in giving a person a firmer grasp of mathematics in general, of making him a better teacher of even plane geometry or introductory algebra. Educationists will further argue that college teachers themselves do not know how or what to teach, for they are the products of the Ph.D. mill which makes them specialists in a very narrow portion of their total discipline. They will argue that education students fail to learn subject matter because the subject-matter professors fail to teach it to them.

No doubt one can cite many horror cases proving this last charge of the educationists (who seem to be taking the offensive now against the colleges, which have long been keeping them on the defensive). I recall a mathematics teacher who could only do calculations, however complicated, in his head, enormously impressing his students, but bewildering them too. There are any number of teachers of English prepared to discourse on the details of Victorian poetry or of medieval literature who are unable to communicate the niceties of sentence structure or the mechanics of punctuation. But these instances are not the result actually of insufficient training in pedagogy. Nor are they the result of the Ph.D. "mill," as has been intimated. They only prove that poor teachers, inflexible and unrealistic, unresponsive to student needs, exist even in college.

It has become fashionable lately to snipe at the Ph.D., which has been called the "union card" for college teaching. The term is derisive but accurate. There are no colleges of first rank which do not require a Ph.D. of their instructors, or the equivalent (and very few accept any equivalent). The degree is described as "Germanic," a mere obstacle course, meaningless in its requirement of original research (many doctoral students do a mechanical exercise), wasteful of the most vital years of the candidate, irrelevant to his ultimate teaching job, destructive of creativity and genuine "originality," and so on. I beg to differ. I would insist that the Ph.D. (or an authentic equivalent) is indispensable to true college teaching.

The Ph.D., ideally, includes a knowledge of a general field as well as intimate acquaintance with a small portion of that field. Thus a man with a Ph.D. in biology knows not only the rudiments of the various branches of biology, but knows very well one subdivision of biology, say, ornithology, and even a subdivision of *that*, say, a particular species of bird. The same is true in English: I am prepared to teach a survey of British literature, from Beowulf to Virginia Woolf; my special period is the seventeenth century; in that century, my specialty is Milton, and particularly Milton in the Restoration. The training of the Ph.D. resembles that of the medical specialist; it is actually a postgraduate degree, and most Ph.D.'s also have the M.A.

I submit there is no substitute for Ph.D. preparation as a requirement for college teaching. True college subjects—calculus, literature, principles of government, European history—are not ends in themselves; they are introductory to full and exhaustive fields. A teacher who knows where calculus leads, who knows the richness beneath the surface of a literature survey or a period of history, can communicate not only the substance of his subject but its implications, its import, its connection with education in general, with civilization, with culture. Wordsworth's "Tintern Abbey," Coleridge's "Kubla Khan," Keats' "Ode on a Grecian Urn" are the surface brilliance of a vast treasure house, which includes not only the full works of each author, but the whole spirit of the Romantic movement, a period in the history of man's ideas and creativity, an era in the development of man's moral and emotional sense. Euclidean geometry is the merest and most pallid introduction to the nature of the physical world, the paradoxes of parallel lines meeting, of Lobachevskian and Riemannian geometry, of the complications and strange truths of topology, of an enclosed universe. Even punctuation and sentence structure cannot be taught properly, that is, other than mechanically, without a sense of the history of English, an instinct for style as an art, and an acquaintance with other languages.

Now it may well be that there are graduate schools where getting the Ph.D. is a routine and stale process, but this is no argument against the Ph.D.; it is merely an indictment of particular schools. But even at the best schools, it will be argued, the discipline required of the Ph.D. is debilitating to imagination and creativity. I say nonsense. No doubt one will find himself accommodating uncomfortably and unwillingly to one or another professor one meets along the arduous way toward the degree, but this sort of accommodation is a matter of yielding to reality; it may even be, in its own sad way, instructive, as one tries to apprehend the whims and the values of an unsympathetic or stupid professor. And within the confines of the ritual, there is much opportunity for exploitation of individual responses, imaginative orientations. Some of our foremost literary personages, Lionel Trilling, Mark Schorer, Joseph Wood Krutch, produced significant work in their dissertations.

The educationists, and others, argue that the emphasis put on research and "publication" in college departments compels a neglect of teaching, a debasing of the simple classroom function to a secondary role. They point out that advancement in colleges depends on continued publication of research and scholarship and not necessarily on the quality of one's teaching. There is no doubt, too, that much that passes for research and scholarship is shabby, trivial, often worthless stuff, comma-counting, pointless collections of data, foolish experiments, and the like. But, again, this is not the ideal, and there is no penalty for publishing worthwhile articles.

It is erroneous to suggest, as critics of college arrangements like to do, that scholarship has no relation to teaching. This is almost malicious, for some of the finest work a college teacher publishes is the result of inspirations developed in the classroom, hypotheses tried out on and with his students, answers to fundamental questions that arose out of the give and take of teaching. Nor do I have in mind advanced work only. There are problems to be considered and ruminated on and fresh answers to be offered, even in introductory courses, although, admittedly, some of the issues here are more pedagogic than scholarly. William Strunk's classic little book on style developed out of his introductory writing classes. Edward Teller has gone back to freshman teaching. At Columbia (Lionel Trilling), Yale (Cleanth Brooks), Harvard (Arthur Schlesinger, Sr. and Jr., David Riesman) great scholars and scientists teach undergraduates *by choice.*

The finest teaching goes hand in hand with scholarship, for the best scholarship is that which is connected with the vitality of the daily teaching task, which illuminates the teaching. My mammalogist friend has done pioneering work classifying the small desert mammals of New Mexico; he publishes his work, he teaches it; a geologist colleague studies the terrain in which uranium deposits may be found and reports his work to his students; a folklorist considers the naming of towns and cities in New Mexico.

Nor should teaching be separated from art, from creativity. To be sure, there are many restrictive, constrictive, destructive forces at work on the artist in the academy, and the hopeful painter, writer, musician must learn to resist these, or at least to accommodate to them, no less firmly than he deals with enemy forces in the world at large. The ideal teacher, of course, is the one who is both scholar and artist. One of my teachers, Ralph Gordon, dedicated a book to one of his teachers, Earl Fenton Palmer, "who never knew the world's need to separate teaching from scholarship, or scholarship from art." Few, very few teachers achieve this glorious synthesis, but many approach it, for a moment here, a moment there, and for all college teachers the combination remains not only an ideal, but a day-to-day possibility. And if art will not grow naturally on the campus, more and more universities will bring art to themselves, hiring Heifetz and Frost and any number of painters and sculptors.

The educationists, who would no doubt like to get all teachers to take their courses, charge that college teachers do not know "how" to teach, that they have never taken courses in the philosophy or psychology or methods of teaching. It is true that there are many different notions of how to teach effectively on the college level. I have known colleagues to assert that no professor should remain behind his desk during a lecture, or in front of the desk, or use a lesson plan, or fail to use one, or lecture without allowing discussion, or allow discussion. Some professors are authoritarian, permitting no student to have an opinion different from their own; some are totally permissive. All that this should prove, however, is not that there is anarchy in college teaching, but that it is possible to teach on the college level without any set of methods, without any rote, without any series of fixed principles.

Teaching in college, surely more than that on primary or secondary levels, is an art, not a science. Kittredge taught by intimidation; Agassiz by throwing a fish skeleton at Shaler and telling him to study it, rejecting as incomplete each report Shaler brought back until Shaler, quite on his own, worked out a great deal about piscatorial anatomy; Christian Gauss by inspiring excitement. I had the good fortune at Columbia to sit in the seminar taught by Jacques Barzun and Lionel Trilling. Barzun was quick and sharp, logical, articulate, brilliant, incisive; Trilling was meditative, slowly reaching for a point, gradually allowing the gears to mesh, and then suddenly bathing the room with a lambent, large, graceful intelligence. Both were superb teachers. College teaching responds to a class, to a student, to a particular situation; it is not ever an automatic matter, not even when the material may be laid out just so, point by point, in a lecture. College teaching is a matter of endless improvisation.

I think it not excessive to suggest that college teachers in a sense do not have to teach, the students have to learn. Let the professor know his subject thoroughly, find it vital and stimulating, and he will not be able to do anything but teach. I remember professors of mine who mumbled to themselves, whose voices were a monotone, whose delivery was dry and dusty, who spoke with thick accents, and who taught me as much as more lively, more expressive lecturers, who were less transported by their subject. The instructor need have only the minimum of skills of expression and voice; the rest is up to the students.

I know well, of course, that the instructor of freshman students must have the talents of a night-club comedian to hold the attention of his students, or of an expert kindergarten teacher, but then we all know that much of freshman teaching is not on the true college level. It is here, I should gladly concede, that some sense and knowledge of "methods," of "educational psychology," of the use of tests, of statistics, would be most helpful. But it is on the freshman level, also, we should not forget, that most instructors begin their college experience and learn much of the practical problems through sheer trial and error, under mature guidance.

College teaching is an art that should not be debased to the level of mere method. I would suggest that the low state of elementary and high-school teaching in this country is at least partly the result of the emphasis on methods. It is taken for granted by too many persons that teaching the third grade is a skill not unlike that of typing, that can be learned in so many semesters at a college of education, and that is, in status and reward, not superior to the status and reward of the typist. Of course, sensible, experienced, objective school administrators know very well that good teaching is an inner quality, like character and wisdom, and not something external, like credits collected in courses. It would be one of the most dangerous blows to higher education in the United States to concede in any way that true college teaching may be reduced to mechanics, fixed by formula, or even to concede that teachers in high school might be able to teach some introductory college courses on their premises. High-school teachers, for all their virtues, teach at the extreme upper limit of their knowledge and capacities; college teachers, when they handle freshman and sophomore courses, teach at the lowest limits of theirs.

Some observers of American higher education have deplored the "elevation" of superior, experienced teachers to administrative posts. They have worried about the tendency of college teachers to seem more and more to want to escape from the classroom, to give up teaching in favor of research or writing or traveling. The better the teacher, the more he has integrated his scholarship or his art with his classroom work, the more likely he is to get a fellowship or a grant or an appointment that calls for little or no appearance in the classroom. Mr. Barzun in his *House of Intellect* and elsewhere has eloquently lamented this trend.

Yet I am persuaded that the situation is not nearly so bad as has been charged; indeed, I think it is good. The only teachers I happen to know who totally gave up their teaching when they were raised to administrative heights were men who were not very happy in the classroom to begin with. I recall one man who taught by rote, could not publish, and did not have the Ph.D. He would have remained an assistant professor to the day of his retirement, but he did happen to be perceptive and not overmodest. He began a campaign to advertise his merits as a teacher, a claim not easily verified, until he found himself removed from the classroom and put in charge of an administrative chore. He was happy, and so were the students. He never went back to the classroom. On the other hand, any number of excellent teachers have found themselves chairmen, deans (Gauss), even presidents (Conant), including Mr. Barzun himself (now provost at Columbia); one way or another, they have found themselves sneaking back to the classroom. The moral here is simple: the good teacher wants to teach. Teaching is a calling with him, not a chore. The good teacher satisfies himself completely only in the classroom. It is only the poor teacher who looks for the first chance to abandon the classroom. Ambition, no doubt, must be served, but so must the needs of self-fulfillment.

I would argue that the poor teacher should be encouraged to get out of the classroom by whatever means possible (he should, ideally, be urged to get out of academic society altogether, although here we get involved with the issue of how to identify good and poor teachers); I would argue as well that good teachers undoubtedly make good academic administrators. Who else but a good teacher knows so well the mysteries, the possibilities, the successes, the failures of the classroom process? Not all good teachers make good administrators, of course, but the best administrator often has been a good teacher and remains one in his work with colleagues and the community. As for losing good teachers to the lures of administration, I think we may reassure ourselves that, in their administrative wisdom, they will find a way of coming back periodically to the classroom.

A similar argument may be made for the good teacher's taking a leave of absence from his classroom for study and research, for rest and recreation. He will return to his teaching much better for the absence. The academic careerist, the operator who specializes in gathering grants and fellowships, one hard upon the other, is often likely to be as indifferent to teaching as the man lusting and maneuvering for administrative advancement. Foundations tend to put their money on sure things; the man who has published or has received one award has a better chance to receive a grant than the most promising but "unproved" applicant. This is unfortunate, for often good teachers, promising scholars and writers, are passed over until they have somehow managed to prove themselves. Early recognition and encouragement often lead to better teaching, more significant publishing, but the good teacher learns soon to live with various realities about his profession, and one of these is the sad fact of the ways of foundations. Of course, too, all the failure to gain a fellowship may mean is that the disappointed applicant may simply have to teach another year instead of tasting the delights of the British Museum, or the Sorbonne, or the Vatican. And, as I have said, teaching never really disturbs the true teacher.

I conclude: college teachers *can* teach. The questions—in relation to the problem of increasing enrollments and the increasing and changing demands for a college education—are: *how* should they teach and *what?* The number of persons properly qualified to teach in college will not increase in anywhere near the proportion necessary to meet the total demands. What new methods may we legitimately introduce without compromising or adulterating the standards and objectives of a traditional college education? Will we be able to teach in huge lecture classes, using public address systems, or by way of television? How should we adjust the curriculum? Should more students be allowed to graduate? Should we permit degrees in a whole range of "new" subjects?

Unfortunately, here as with so many other crucial social issues, the answers offered relate to larger political, sociological, and philosophical positions. An educationist I know asked me in all seriousness whether I didn't think a college degree was the right of every American citizen. Another colleague asked me whether I would keep from getting a degree anyone who merely couldn't pass a college course in mathematics, or a college course in language.

I confess that I do not understand the rationale of such questions. I do not see that every American has the guaranteed right to a college degree any more than he has such a right to be made a millionaire. Education is education, and while we may define the contents variously, substituting, say, one language for another, one social science for another, this literature course for that one, I do not see how we can throw out fundamental areas simply to accommodate persons with certain incapacities. It really is not catastrophic to go through life without a college degree, any more than it is not to be a millionaire. It would be catastrophic to water down curriculum to the point where a degree is worthless.

Although I urge a conservative and traditional response to curriculum in the face of the tidal wave of students and the demand for universal degrees, I also urge unconventional ways of meeting the wave in terms of technique. There is nothing sacred about teaching students in classes of small number and by ancient methods and requiring a fixed number of courses. While television will certainly never be effective in some subjects (freshman English, I venture, for example), there are a number of subjects which can surely be taught as effectively via television as in the classroom. Any television teaching offers problems, no doubt, not least those connected with broadcasting on an open channel with the public at large tuning in and possibly inhibiting the teacher with its censorious eye and mind. All sorts of subjects may be taught quite successfully in larger classes than are now thought possible. Some of the best courses at Columbia and Harvard are taught with audiences of 100 or 200. Both schools also emphasize quality and depth of learning, not quantity of credits.

But while we try out "mass production" methods, we should also maintain small, "hand crafted" methods where necessary. Certain advanced courses cannot be taught to large numbers of students, even were large numbers interested in taking such courses, for example, as crystallography, or Greek, or Old English. But all of the necessary adjustments will be made *ad hoc*, as the occasions arise.

The history of college education in the United States—in the world, for that matter—proves perhaps one thing without question, that its nature has changed with changing needs. It has accommodated to new and meaningful demands, admitted new subjects to the curriculum, meeting new problems as they arose. We have no "golden age" of universities, I venture, and I do not think we must commit ourselves irrevocably to the present period as though every change is a loss, a step down towards disaster. The habitual complainers of the past must have lamented the passing of the Doctor of Divinity or the Bachelor of Philosophy degrees, as much as some persons today bemoan the passing of Latin. I cite Latin because I happen to think of myself as something of a Latinist, and I still argue that Latin is one of the valuable components of a liberal education. But I would not tie a liberal education simply to Latin alone; it includes a complex of subjects, certainly, but any one might be sacrificed without significantly adulterating the complex. Indeed one might sacrifice the authentic meaning of a liberal education by an intransigent, ritualistic adherence to any particular subject.

As American higher education is attacked by lowbrows, vulgarians, ritualistic conformists and nonconformists, educationists, even as it is defended by the sort of friends who do more harm than good, we may console ourselves not only by the lesson of history, but by the amorphous, sprawling, vast, undefinable, various conglomeration our colleges and universities constitute today. Somewhere in this huge landscape, someone, somehow, will be defending the local citadel against the local enemies, with tactics adjusted to the immediate terrain. It is in this multitude of defense actions that the salvation of our colleges lies. So long as teachers stick to their teaching, students to their studies, the larger aspects will ultimately—that is, in the context of history—surely take care of themselves.

number of students in the population who want to go to college. "In 1941," he writes, "Amherst, for example, had 371 applicants for 232 openings, while Princeton had 925 for 644. Today, Princeton has 3,213 applicants for 757 places, and Amherst chooses among 1,677 applicants to fill its 259 openings." Each year in the sixties, the Ivy League schools expect an increase of twenty percent in applications over the year before. Colleges inevitably had to add scholastic ability as a criterion for admission even if Sputnik had never raised the outcry to improve American college scholarship.

Of course, the changing attitudes in our society about discrimination, the cancelling of quotas against Jews and other groups, have also helped raise the intellectual level of colleges: if "social" criteria could no longer be the sole or main ones applied (students with approved social credentials increased in the population in about as large numbers as all students), then scholastic aptitude had to become more significant. And certainly as the pressures for attending prestige colleges developed, it would have been insane to keep applying more and more restrictive, "snobbish" screening standards. Harvard might soon have been attended only by the Lowells and Cabots.

That the "prestige" colleges should try to maintain their prestige, in terms of the current conceptions of prestige, is not at all surprising. It is gratifying and surprising, however, to find that state universities, committed in theory to the wholesale and "democratic" welcoming of all high-school graduates in the state, regardless of their talents or attainments, should devote so much time, energy, and expense to the careful selection and the expensive teaching of superior students. Indeed, one whole and immense branch of the California college system, the university at Berkeley, is already well on the way to making its *entire* student body an elite corps; students with less than a certain minimum high-school performance simply enroll in one of the many California state colleges.

What we are involved in as a nation, in spite of all complaints and laments to the contrary, is the raising of intellectual pursuit to the level once occupied by football heroes and campus queens. At any number of places, fraternities and sororities seek out students with superior grades in genuine academic subjects as eagerly as they once solicited athletes. Just as the prestige colleges constitute an elite, as Berkeley students are an elite, so honors students are an elite at those campuses with honors programs.

Honors programs operate in all sorts of different ways. Some are merely departmental, some start only in the third year, some are extracurricular. I am most familiar with the program at the University of New Mexico, which was among the first schools in the country to establish a four-year all-university program. In effect, the program constitutes a new "college" within the university.

In their first year at the University of New Mexico, the honors students register in a colloquium, in groups of not more than fifteen, with two professors from different disciplines. The students and professors read a book a week, selected by the professors from paperback catalogues, and talk about it. Typical titles are: *The Basic Ideas of Hamilton, The Wealth of Nations, Huckleberry Finn, Howard's End, Gulliver's Travels, The Organization Man, The Opinions of Learned Hand.* In their sophomore year, the students enroll in two seminars, one each semester, in subjects outside their expected field of specialization. These seminars are limited to ten students. In the junior year, the survivors go on to an intensive survey of Western religion, drama, painting, political science, and physical science. In the senior year, they are assigned to individual research projects in their major departments and meet again weekly for a discussion period. Some seniors will pair off with professors to conduct freshman colloquia. All students, of course, also follow the normal curriculum.

The attrition rate is high. The sixty starting freshmen diminish by a third at the end of the first year. High-school grades and test performance have proven inadequate measures for success in honors. Some of the best college students, unrecognized earlier, show up at the end of the freshman year; these are welcomed into the program. But even with this additional recruitment, there may be only a dozen or fifteen students finishing the full four-year program. A rigorous attempt is made to maintain quality; the minimum grade average for remaining in the program rises every year until in the fourth year it is close to straight A.

In addition to providing four full years of work for honors students, the U.N.M. program is also unusual in allowing full teaching credit to faculty for all honors courses (two professors for fifteen freshmen is one of the richest such allotments in the country), offering courses in all university disciplines (the U.N.M. School of Law, for example, is directing a sophomore seminar), offering students full course credit for honors work (but without materially reducing the usual number of credits required by standard curricula), and in giving advanced honors students generous financial allowances (for need) and rewards (for achievement).

There is no doubt that as the program establishes itself more and more firmly, and clears up problems, honors students at U.N.M. will eventually be getting as good a college education as they could get anywhere in the country. By separating the honors students in their own classes (in addition to the colloquia, honors freshmen also take their English courses as a group), encouraging competition and friendship among them, providing opportunities for close contacts with faculty, the program offers students all of the "non-academic" advantages of enrollment in one of the small prestige colleges. All this, it must be remembered, at a public university of medium size in a poor state.

The honors program does not try to teach anything specific. The students learn their subject matter in their regular courses, in English, economics, history, physics, engineering, nursing. The honors courses try to develop a sense of the vastness, depths, subtleties, pleasures, complexities, interrelations of man's achievements in knowledge and art. They try to teach the students to respond to all sorts of intellectual and emotional prodding, and to have confidence in their responses, a confidence appropriately modulated by humility. The worst sort of instructor for honors is the one who dictates opinions, judgments, tastes, who does not encourage these to rise out of the students themselves. Hopefully, the aim of honors is to turn out a student who knows both how much he knows and how little, the mark of any liberally educated person.

At the University of North Carolina, a sophomore honors student recently explained to a group of alumni some of the ends of honors work. Here are excerpts from his address: "First there must begin in the classroom a dialogue—a dialogue between professor and student, between student and student, but most importantly between the student and himself. . . . This dialogue must begin in the classroom, but it must extend into the entire life of the student—into dormitory and fraternity, into social life and religious life, into his other classes and his extracurricular activities . . . the student should be thrown into a state of creative tension in which the foundations for the only valid security can be laid, that security which rests on individual thought."

Honors is an obvious boon to the many able students throughout the country who cannot possibly expect to go to Amherst, Harvard, Yale, Columbia, Williams, Vassar, Wellesley, Stanford, if only because they do not have the money to pay the expensive tuitions. And even if they do have the money, more and more will be turned away simply because there will be no room. Certainly state universities have a responsibility to educate all students in their state, the best as well as the poorest.

As significant as the advantages offered to honors students themselves is the continuous intellectual stimulation provided to everyone on campus by a solidly established honors program. The honors students mingle with other students in all of their non-honors courses, and honors faculty keep teaching their regular assignments. It is impossible for the intellectual liveliness, the mental passion, of honors students and professors not to spread out widely on the campus at large. One way or another, every student, every professor is affected, even those who oppose honors programs for personal or ideological reasons. (Some object to honors programs because they are "undemocratic.")

There is scarcely a college in the country today that does not have or is not planning a program for superior students in one form or another. What this means is that while preparing for incoming hordes of students, American higher education is not neglecting to prepare for the very small contingents among them of outstanding students. The Carnegie Foundation has established the Inter-University Committee on the Superior Student to encourage the setting-up of honors programs in every type of college and university, from the small liberal arts schools to the large engineering institutions. Clearly the United States is not sacrificing quality to the god of quantity.

It means also that we are not establishing narrow "training" assembly lines, such as those which exist in Russia, which "train" an engineer or a mathematician or a physicist. In spite of the lamentations of an Admiral Rickover, American education has clearly committed itself to turning out scientists who will not be ignorant of poetry or sociology or the felicities of style; humanists who will have a good notion of the history and nature of science. The honors programs throughout the country, whatever momentary failures or shortcomings may appear here or there, are incontrovertible, overwhelming evidence that American higher education, in spite of what some sour critics say to the contrary, is meeting, on at least one major front, its full responsibility.

THIRTEEN

THE LIMITS OF INTELLECT

INTELLECTUALS are both culture heroes and culture villains in our time. On television, we will turn from one program on which the bespectacled highbrow is an object of derision (sometimes quite affectionately so, especially when he is made an amiable freak), to another on which he is an object of worship. We have had Wally Cox as "Mr. Peepers," a good-natured, awkward, bumbling high-school teacher of science, with all sorts of esoteric interests, and Charles Van Doren as himself, which is to say a combination of Charlton Heston and Gregory Peck in the college classroom. The high-domed announcers like Tony Marvin on the Godfrey programs, or Frank Gallup with Perry Como or Milton Berle, or Hugh Downs with Jack Paar, with their polysyllabic and orotund gibberish, are supposed to pass as signs of ridiculous high learning. They are balanced by such oracular yet casual personages, openly exhibiting their erudition and private wit, as Clifton Fadiman, John Daly, Bennett Cerf, intended to elicit respect.

Whether the great mass audience in the United States

is supposed to respect or deride intellectuals does not matter so much as the fact that it is supposed to separate itself from them. Intellectuals may be good guys or bad guys, but they are always *those* guys, never ourselves. This is so not only in television but in the movies, in the mass-circulation magazines (the *Saturday Evening Post* occasionally runs stories in which the villain can be promptly recognized by the Ivy League suit he is described as wearing and the university he is said to have graduated from), and in public life. President Eisenhower was expected at least once during a press conference to say something like "I am no expert but . . ." Few politicians want to risk the appellation of "egghead," to indicate knowledge of anything less (or more) substantial than business or military affairs.

Whatever ambivalent place intellectuals may occupy in our culture at large, for nonconformists they are always pure heroes. Indeed, many nonconformists would undoubtedly insist that they do not conform precisely because they are intellectual. No form of organized nonconformism today fails to identify itself with intellectualism. Even the most illiterate beatnik confesses to an admiration of poetry, music, and art, at least certain types of each, and comes to his anti-intellectual philosophy of Zen through some operation of the mind. But it is in the more respectable, more "middle class" centers of nonconformism that intellectual activity, the exercise of apparent taste or judgment, the making of distinctions, the assertion of certainty, the observance of taboos are taken to be of the essence of nonconformity. For how else does one attain to the enlightenment of nonconformity except through thought? It is, after all, the mindless masses and Babbitts who accept what everyone else accepts and conform to it automatically, thoughtlessly, who demonstrate that conformity is to be equated with lack of intellect and even with opposition to intellect.

I have no doubt that it is better to work with the mind in responding to the world than without it; it is better to be "intellectual," that is, than anti-intellectual. But one of the penalties intellectuals often have to pay for being what they are is the surrender of a breadth of vision, a catholicity of understanding, the suspension of a continuously active sense of taste and judgment. Having taken the initial and, for them, seemingly daring step of declaring themselves intellectuals, all subsequent steps and gestures are likely to follow a ritualistic, automatic pattern.

What else can account for the adulation in which intellectuals held Charles Van Doren (before the exposé, of course) when he was performing his prodigious mental calisthenics on television? College teachers, television critics, the readers of books and book reviews all believed, as Van Doren himself apparently did, that his performances actually had something to do with intellect, that his popularity was encouraging an interest in learning. It was enough simply for him *to appear* to be intellectual. "According to Van Doren's Washington testimony," John Ciardi wrote in the *Saturday Review*, "one of [the producer's] most telling arguments in urging the deception was that Van Doren, as the bearer of a well-known literary name and as college teacher, 'would increase public respect for the intellectual life and for the teaching profession.'"

We all knew better then, and of course we know better now. Spieling off the names and details of the wives of Henry VIII, giving the dates of the battles of the Civil

War, locating World War II engagements in the Pacific, have little to do with learning or intellect. Electronic computers and Teddy Nadlers can certainly do any of these things, after the information has been fed in, at least as well as a carefully coached college instructor. Yet no self-respecting intellectual would confuse the operations of an IBM machine or of Mr. Nadler with intellectual activity, in Mr. Nadler's case perhaps only because he did not present the image of an intellectual at work, while of course Mr. Van Doren did.

For all his superiority about his sense of discrimination, the intellectual often responds principally to surface appearances. This is one reason, perhaps, why the announcers who appear on CBS television news programs and who look like Hollywood reporters—Edward R. Murrow, Eric Sevareid, Howard K. Smith, Winston Burdette—used to impress most intellectuals much more than the more ordinary-looking reporters at the time on NBC. CBS reporters were constantly appearing in such "intellectual" journals as *The Reporter, The Nation, The Saturday Review.* Perhaps it was in reaction to this glamorous image projected by CBS newsmen that a *New York Times* staff member once insisted in a discussion with me that NBC offers far better coverage of news than CBS. This was before NBC got its own crew of glamorous pundits, Chet Huntley, David Brinkley, Frank McGee. It must be this unbalanced response to appearance alone that is at the source of the frequent offers Edward R. Murrow gets to become a college president. He looks and sounds like the intellectual nonconformist's idea of a college president, in the company, of course, of Robert M. Hutchins and Harold Taylor.

Intellectuals—as much as nonintellectuals and anti-intellectuals—prefer to respond to a sure thing. It is easier on the mind to know that a book we are going to read is good because the author has been certified as good, or a movie we're going to see is so, or a play, or a record, or a painting. If a college president turns out to be a flop, we might as well have a man that looks like a college president; no sense having someone flop as a president who, in the bargain, doesn't look like one. To the extent that the Broadway theater is still patronized by intellectuals, the operation of "the law of the sure thing" for intellectuals can be seen very clearly there. A Lerner and Loewe production, or a play by Tennessee Williams or William Inge, or a play offering the Lunts is likely to be sold out for months (sometimes years) *in advance of the actual opening.* We don't even have to read the critics to know the work is "good," to know that we are going to like it. A book by Faulkner is guaranteed a certain minimum sale; a painting by Picasso cannot be bad; a recording by Leonard Bernstein must be a hit.

Perhaps in matters of art the law of the sure thing has some justification. Any book by William Faulkner, however bad in certain ways, is bound to have a considerable degree of interest; any painting by Picasso should offer the viewer some kind of edification. The law operates perniciously only when it excludes a response to unfamiliar, new, unsure things. I am not concerned here with the problem of the young and struggling artist obtaining recognition; perseverance, talent, tirelessness, dedication, intelligence, I am old-fashioned enough to believe, will one way or another bring their reward.

The law operates perniciously in larger and more impersonal areas. Consider the years it took for the movies to receive appropriate intellectual appreciation, to be considered on the basis of the same serious esthetic standards we take for granted with books and with plays (not that we always see such standards applied for the latter). Movies were simply not a sure thing; indeed, they were the opposite, especially if made in the United States: American movies as a class were—and in some circles still are—thought to be surely bad, *a priori* "commercial" and inartistic. The lyrics of popular songs are where movies were several decades ago and may never be anywhere else. Television is a naughty word not even brought up in intellectual circles.

The law of the sure thing works in all areas of American intellectual life. A number of foundations sponsor the work of "promising" young artists. But mere "promise" can never be a sure thing. What critic, what expert, will risk his status to bet on someone who might turn out well when he can so easily confirm his status by betting on someone who *has* turned out well in the past? If you have already made a name, you are much more likely to receive a fellowship or a grant than if you are simply in the process of establishing a name. One thinks of Johnson's dismissal of Lord Chesterfield when the latter offered to patronize Johnson only after his reputation was firmly established.

We see the reluctance, the hesitation, the timidity of intellect to pierce beyond the borders of what is certain in all sorts of intellectual strongholds. Many university departments of literature do not include courses in contemporary writing, concluding their offerings with the nineteenth century, or, if they are very bold, with one or two figures who lived into the twentieth. After all, we are sure of the place of Tennyson and Browning, but how can we tell yet about Yeats or Eliot, especially Eliot, who is actually still living? It is rare indeed that experi-

the way of the ultra-logical scientists who people Huxley's and Wells' novels, the men who exclude all other human dimensions but that of the mind; but there is nothing inherent in intellectualism which requires an exclusion of the emotional or spiritual or esthetic. Throughout history intellectuals of various types have comfortably embodied the opposing tendencies of logic and emotion, of science and esthetics.

We can find excuses, extenuations, rationalizations for the intellectual. The nonintellectual, after all, can skim all areas of experience; the surfaces of things content him. The intellectual, however, inevitably immerses himself in one area or one group of areas, and he may sometimes not even be conscious of the rest of the world. Einstein's innocence of all sorts of contemporary subjects was notorious. Many persons who make their living in intellectual pursuits and must spend their evenings reading do not own television sets and consequently are quite ignorant of the immense half-world of popular entertainment. A sociologist friend of mine once asked at a party, "Who is this man Liberace I keep reading about?" He pronounced the name "Liber-ace," the "ace" as in poker. As a sociologist he had been instrumental in contributing to perhaps the most important change in our time in the study of society. No doubt there was no need at all for him specifically to know Liberace, or any other popular entertainer, in his work, but mass culture does touch, if only tangentially, on his domain. It happens that he was not unaware of his limitation and was amused by it and determined to overcome it as best he could. On the other hand, I heard one of the country's most prominent and subtle "critics of our culture" declare at a public meeting, in answer to a question, that he never went to the movies (which even now strikes me as rhetorical exaggeration). How can one be any sort of "critic of our culture," on whatever rarefied plain, without ever going to the movies?

Professor Lionel Trilling, of Columbia, is considered by many to be one of the two or three foremost intellectuals of our country, and I may say that I quite agree with this estimate. One finds in his essays the finest achievements of a rich and subtle and large intellect at work, as well as some of the limitations. The literary intellectual, Mr. Trilling once wrote, "seems to find more and more difficulty in believing that there is a significant reality to be found in anything except literature itself . . . or in believing that any profession save that of literature is interesting and deserves credence." Mr. Trilling's remarks come from an essay he contributed to a symposium in *Partisan Review* on "The Situation of the American Intellectual at the Present Time." In that same essay, listing some of the areas of ignorance of the American intellectual, Mr. Trilling asks: "Who amongst us has any adequate idea about the quality of the teaching staffs of the schools? What is the literary curriculum of our high schools? What is taught in 'Social Studies'? What actually happens in a 'progressive' school—I mean apart from what everybody jokes about? What happens in colleges?"

Mr. Trilling is quite right in indicating the blind spots of so many American intellectuals, but he misses one under his own eye. Professor David Daiches, who is by way of being a British literary intellectual himself, answers Mr. Trilling in the course of an essay in *Commentary*, "The Mind of Lionel Trilling." "Certainly, here at Indiana University," Mr. Daiches says, "where I am at the moment Visiting Professor, I have found few of my colleagues who do not know, and who are not actively concerned about, what is being taught and how it is being taught in the high schools and teachers' colleges of the state. I could have a good shot myself at telling Mr. Trilling what is taught in 'Social Studies,' what actually happens in a 'progressive' school, and what is the literary curriculum of at least some high schools." Mr. Daiches attributes Mr. Trilling's limitations to his being "a metropolitan intellectual," working principally on the basis of data that "have all been written about. He knows more about the intellectual atmosphere of Cambridge, England, than of Bloomington, Indiana: the former has been written about. Trilling's mind will play luminously with what he knows, and what he knows is what has a *literature*."

Mr. Trilling's sensibility is so capacious, his sensitivity to forces and backgrounds so acute, that he comes closer to embracing a total reality with all his "metropolitan" limitations than the most indefatigably alert American intellectual of the "provinces." The metropolis, at least, as Mr. Daiches points out, requires the intellectual to be sophisticated, undoctrinaire, and "untainted with snobbism." I have seen intellectuals in the provinces, as I am sure Mr. Daiches has, whose intellectualism is quite the reverse of these things, whose smugness is as invincible as their ignorance.

But the fact remains that even the most unbigoted intellectual at some point reveals an incapacity to apprehend some significant area of experience. No doubt, again, it is a matter of specialization; to be intellectual means to make choices among possible interests, to exclude certain ones for the sake of concentration on a few. But often unawareness is made a point of principle.

Jacques Barzun, Mr. Trilling's close friend and colleague at Columbia University, has on a number of occasions wondered what has happened to intellectual life in America that conversation is no longer practiced as it was in "the good old days." Aside from the question of just how bright and civilized conversation at large was in some Golden Age of the past, I wonder whether it is fair or meaningful to denigrate a social poker evening or chamber-music session or bridge party by comparison with an evening of talk. Gatherings where talk is at a minimum, confined to trivial essentials, offer their own rich if intangible satisfactions, certainly of a different nature from those deriving from talk but perhaps of a similar intense order. Intellectuals tend to exalt the virtues of conversation, but the chatter that passes for talk at gatherings of certified intellectuals—at cocktail parties or at the dinner table or in the living room—can often be as much a means of evading a probing engagement with truth as a bridge party. Our time has not been slack in keeping up the art of talk perhaps, so much as it has been ingenious in inventing reasons for social gatherings where pure talk would be held to a minimum, or put in a subordinate relation to social maneuvering.

I wonder, too, whether the drawing rooms of Congreve and Wycherley and Austen and Wilde better satisfied the human need to gather in groups than contemporary bridge parties do. Indeed, a bridge or poker competition may well meet the need to do something with somebody else much better than a conversational contest, an exchange of epigrams, or an alternating series of pontifical pronouncements. No doubt an extended conversational encounter between persons of high seriousness, both equally articulate, both honest and more interested in the direction of a conversation than in shooting off fireworks along the way, is an intellectually more worthy enterprise than the most *gemütlich* card game or musical meeting, but such encounters have always been rare and will continue to be. I think it is intellectually sentimental to lament the "passing" of such conversation, or its paucity today.

Conversation, or at least what is thought to be conversation, is another "metropolitan" art. It is in the big city that the art of appearing to talk while saying nothing has been most highly cultivated. Conversation here is often precisely the best way of not conversing. John Cheever has a harrowing story of a skilled but socially inept surgeon who after marrying a "fashionable" lady applied his prodigious analytical skill to determining the best way of making his way in New York society. He concluded that memorizing certain conversational gambits, inversions of all sorts of clichés, for example, would guarantee social success. Then, one evening at a cocktail party, tired after a day at the hospital, head swollen with alcohol, he gets all of the pat gambits confused, begins to sound wildly drunk, even insane, and is led, gibbering his inanities, from the party.

It is in the country at large, in smaller cities, in towns, where one cannot run off at will to the theater or to a concert or to a lecture, where one cannot casually and quickly get together a large gathering of glibly chattering friends and colleagues, that the small and patient social pleasures of picnics and bridge parties and poker sessions and aimless sessions of sweet, silent drinking are nurtured.

In the big city, one follows a formula to make contact; protocol is endless: telephone calls before the casual visit; a fixed and rigid system of reciprocity of dinner and cocktail invitations; the steady revising of lists of persons who cannot be invited simultaneously to the same affair; a consciousness of delicate subjects that cannot be brought up. Intellectual conversation in the big city is enmeshed in the nets of urban civilization. One may not have as many opportunities in the small city for launching into big and serious talk, it is true, but there are more chances for uninhibited, small, light, inconsequential talk. Talking about the weather, about the children, about one's garden, about local politics become ways of engaging socially, of feeling oneself part of a community, of fighting off alienation and loneliness.

Intellectuals tend to talk big, but they also tend to abandon their responsibilities, both the large and the small ones: Businessmen are so stupid and benighted, it isn't worth exerting one's energies trying to communicate with them. Politicians are so petty and corrupt, intellectuals shouldn't soil themselves by descending to their level. The common world is so common, it isn't worth trying to improve; all it's good for is to be insulted, condemned, wiped out. An article in *Harper's* a number of years ago urged that "we should not get out the vote" on the grounds that too many persons did not know how to vote correctly. Among the persons who care least about the specific character of the immediate political situation are intellectuals. Many vote by rote, if they deign to vote at all. They are automatic liberals. It is as difficult to imagine an intellectual troubling to find out enough about the inner details of a particular political situation to the point where he might switch his party vote as it is to imagine any of our intellectual periodicals changing *their* political coloration. Dwight Macdonald announced in *Commentary* that he was not going to vote at all in 1960. This picture may be hyperbole, but it's really very hard to imagine a Republican intellectual, even in Vermont, and I say this after having actually met one in that state.

Essentially, intellectuals are discontent with what they are. Their grousing is often quite unrelated to reality. They complain that intellectuals are not respected in America, yet opinion studies show that the intellectual professions are ranked near the top of any list of American jobs, somewhere in the neighborhood of Supreme Court justices. They complain that intellectual activities are not rewarded appropriately; here, too, studies show that intellectual incomes, even for college professors, are substantially higher than average. What American intellectuals lust for, as Professor S. Martin Lipset, University of California sociologist, has pointed out, is that fantastically lofty status of European intellectuals, which requires that professors' wives be called "Mrs. Professor." Democratic to their bone, American intellectuals would be content only with the adulation once bestowed on nobility.

Dogmatically respectful of intelligence, intellectuals sneer at any type of intelligence that does not manifest itself in the traditional, fashionable ways. Business or political or mechanical or day-to-day intelligence is derided. When intellectuals want to praise the president of a corporation or a public official, they report that he reads the right books or collects the proper paintings or, as was reported in *Harper's* about a Republican Secretary of the Treasury, that he writes memoranda in blank verse. Intellectuals will simultaneously revere and sneer at a shrewd handyman.

Intellectuals have a ritualistic way of demonstrating their status that requires no explanation. Carrying the approved little magazine or journal, dropping the current fashionable phrase or name, displaying the right books (never, perish the thought, a Book of the Month Club selection) and newspapers (a Sunday *New York Times* is essential, but it must always be referred to with a sneer), are positive gestures.

Refusing to wear a Phi Beta Kappa key, never hanging diplomas or signed photographs of the great on one's walls, never watching television—these are negative signs. All the negative signs, however, must be established by positive declarations. After all, what's the point of not wearing a Phi Beta Kappa key if no one knows you are a member? "Look at that bumpkin with the key on his vest," you chuckle in superiority. "I never wear mine! Don't even know where the key is." (Of course, there is good reason for the Phi Beta Kappa key to have sunk into disrepute: so many "intellectuals" could offer the key as their only sign of status and made it finally seem a sure declaration of an empty intellectualism that had stopped at commencement and lived only on undergraduate glory.)

As for diplomas, especially beyond the baccalaureate, these are normally hung in toilets. I have seen doctorate diplomas from New York University and Harvard displayed opposite the one seat in the home where you can't escape studying them closely. Both belonged to enormously earnest intellectuals. This way, of course, you can display and deprecate your status at the same time, mixing humility with pride.

Many intellectuals lack taste. One of the doctoral intellectuals I mentioned above had a home furnished with gaudy Grand Rapids waterfall furniture, "overstuffed" modern chairs and sofas, as well as wrought iron-and-walnut "Danish-type" things from Gimbel's basement. Faculty lounges at most campuses are fashion shows in reverse—of dowdiness, of cheapness, of indifference to the most elementary rules of appearance, of ostentation instead of simplicity, of color clashes, of shabbiness that testifies not to low income but to low apprehension. Learned journals are largely repositories of grubby prose and trivial conclusions, however recondite.

One wonders finally whether intellectualism as a way of life really has essentially to do with the mind, with intelligence or with sensitivity, with taste or judgment, with cultivation or thought. Too many teachers, editors, advertising men, publishers' assistants, lawyers, physicians are merely well-trained, high-grade clerks, whose intellectual orthodoxy, instead of requiring regular attendance at Sunday chapel, requires only the mumbo-jumbo mumbling or exhibition of the totems of current intellectualism.

Those who live in Bohemia have their own uniforms, their own statements of orthodoxy. Some, of course, may be every bit as intelligent as any successful nonintellectual businessman or craftsman, but the intelligence is incidental, not necessary to the practice of the particular form of intellectualism chosen. Patronize the fashionable coffee house and you don't have to say a word identifying yourself, intelligent or otherwise. Announce that you are a painter or a poet, and your claim to estheticism is proved; you are a *maker* of beauty, not a conformist simply enjoying it passively in your living room or in your mirror.

In the twenties, persons in the know used to deride the "bourgeoisie," the society of Babbitts, as a class with fixed habits of thought and feeling and response. It wasn't a precise classification, of course, since so many individuals spilled over the boundaries. But it was meaningful enough. It seems to me that in our time "intellectual" has become a similarly meaningful designation, with all it suggests of achievements, limitations, and exceptions.

FOURTEEN

VIVE LES DIFFÉRENCES!

WRITING about the Jew in the sixth decade of the twentieth century poses problems that would have been thought imaginary just ten years earlier. Indeed, the whole troubled landscape of minority relations within the entire American culture has changed dramatically. With the exception of the unique Puerto Rican problem in New York, one that has developed only lately, the key word for relations of different groups is integration. Even in the South, only die-hards oppose integration forever and without qualification; everyone else opposes certain degrees of integration, opposes immediate or early integration. For Jews, Negroes, Puerto Ricans, Indians, Mexicans, Irish, Poles, the object is assimilation, the blending together of all differences, the leveling-down of all those high spots in the American topography that used to distinguish one group from another.

We see this vividly in the disappearance of certain types of jokes. What Catskill-type comedian, appearing before the most assertively Jewish audience, would think of telling the story about the little Negro boy named Izzy

Goldstein? "Oh no," the boy explains to his teacher, "I'm not Jewish. I've got enough *tzuris* being a *schwarze*." ("I've got enough trouble being Negro.")

In the forties I took a trip around Manhattan Island in a sight-seeing boat. As we passed Yeshivah University, the only general institution of higher learning sponsored by Orthodox Jews in America, the barker told the story of the Irish boy from the Bronx who insisted on going to Yeshivah with his best friend, an Orthodox Jewish boy who lived next door in their apartment house. They shared a room in a Yeshivah dormitory. During the winter recess, the Irish boy returned home, dressed like his Jewish friend, in a long coat, flat European hat, and with long curling sideburns. When his mother saw him, she reared back and jeered: "Look, Joe College himself."

Friends who repeated this sight-seeing trip in the late fifties with the same barker reported that he had eliminated this story when passing Yeshivah. My guess is that it would have puzzled his listeners. For not only have Yeshivah students come to dress like other college students in New York, but the extreme Orthodox sects that have settled in Brooklyn have also started accommodating to the environment. A recent article in *Commentary* described some boys, released for recess from the local synagogue, shooting basketball, calling to each other in Yiddish.

The process of assimilation, of course, has been going on for a long time, ever since there were different groups which felt the need to blend with one another. Surely the problems of assimilation in New Orleans or in San Antonio were no different in the nineteenth century from those in New York, Boston, and Philadelphia in the twentieth; they may have been less intense, smaller in scale, but not different in kind. If one didn't clearly recognize a French or a Mexican or an Irish or a Jewish face, one certainly recognized an accent or a name. We are still making distinctions of this sort, even today, in the great age of assimilation, although perhaps without any invidious intent.

But sometimes the cutting away of differences offers farcical results. One year while he was training at Grossinger's, an assertively Jewish vacation paradise in the Catskills, Rocky Marciano, the Italian heavyweight champion, was asked to help sell Rabbi Phillip Bernstein's book *What the Jews Believe* by autographing copies. Needless to say, the book sold out very quickly.

It is inevitable, of course, that the son and the grandson and the great-grandson of the immigrant of the late 1800's and early 1900's should look more like the "typical American" than his parents. Senator John Kennedy and Governor Abe Ribicoff are not to be distinguished on first glance from gentlemen in finance or advertising outfitted by the same Ivy League clothiers. Yet there is still a lingering wish to place someone "ethnically," by origin, in terms of family. There's the story of the nice grandmotherly Jewish lady who found herself on a plane next to a distinguished-looking man, complete with Homburg, vest, and attaché case, busy shuffling his papers.

"Excuse me," she said to him, "I know you are a busy man. But tell me something. I hope you won't mind. Are you Jewish?"

The man looked up, smiled thinly, and answered, "No, madame, I'm not," and went back to his papers.

The lady nodded, shrugged, was silent for a while, then nudged him again. "Are you sure you're not Jewish? After all, you don't have to be ashamed. Not with me."

The man smiled and answered shortly. "No, I'm not

Jewish."

"So all right," the lady said. After a while, however, unable to contain herself, she turned to him again. "Absolutely not?" she asked. "You're sure, absolutely, you're not Jewish?"

The man gave up. "Madame," he turned to her with a flourish, "I am Jewish. I am. Now may I get back to my work?"

The lady settled herself contentedly. "You know something," she said, "you don't look it at all."

The lady's satisfaction that the man did *not* look Jewish is at the heart of so much of Jewish life today. While Jews do not want to be excluded from certain residential areas, or from country or social clubs, they do not, as a group, really want to join them. They want their own clubs, their own residential areas, which will *look like* every one else's. The ladies at Grossinger's dress like those at Newport or Palm Springs or the Riviera (or wherever our new international rich go), with the latest "frocks" and the latest mutations in minks, but on Friday nights, they will raise their expensive coats over their heads, perch on their high-heeled shoes, and say the traditional Sabbath blessings over the candles. And when the Sabbath is broken the next night, they will cha-cha-cha in the ballroom.

Throughout the country, the object is to have the temple look like the Protestant chapel, the rabbi like the minister. Indeed, Protestant ministers frequently exchange pulpits with rabbis. The temple and the synagogue have become principally social centers. Perhaps the story is apocryphal of the synagogue committee questioning an applicant who wanted to be the new rabbi as to his knowledge of bridge and poker rather than of Talmud and Jewish history, but it illustrates one expectation congregations have about their rabbi. He is not to be principally their leader in belief, in study, in prayer; he is to be an exalted kind of "community social worker," knowledgeable in bridge, poker, golf and the intricacies of running plays, dinners, fashion shows, luncheons, "book reviews," and other such social affairs. Indeed, many of the large Jewish congregations do hire professional community social workers. Nor is this tendency to emphasize the communal aspect of Jewish life, an entirely legitimate emphasis of course, limited only to Jews. I understand other groups make a similar complaint: that attendance at affairs sponsored by churches is motivated by social reasons first, religious reasons last, or hardly at all.

In an attempt to wipe out the nasty aspects of religious differences, we start first by making jokes, then by insisting there are no differences at all, then, finally, by indeed wiping out differences. It used to and may still be a great joke among night club and television comedians to say that Manischewitz wine is used in Catholic ritual. Manischewitz wine, of course, carries the name of one of the oldest, most rigidly Orthodox Jewish firms in the United States, which built its reputation on making matzohs, the unleavened bread used during Passover by Jews. I find this sort of joke almost as irritating as a crazy lady's attack on one of the leading detergents for carrying the seal of approval, the "U" within an "O," of the Union of Orthodox Hebrew Congregations, signifying that nothing in the ingredients is unkosher, and that the product may safely be used by the most Orthodox Jew. She complained that priests might be washing their vestments, and I suppose ministers their Brooks Brothers shirts, in what she called "kosher soap."

It seems to me as frivolous to complain about "kosher"

the various sects in Protestantism, and even the primitive religions of the American Southwest, the Far East, and Africa, the facts still remain: there are crucial cultural, doctrinal, historical, philosophical differences, and it should be healthy and good that these differences are not only recognized but, in some cases, preserved. Differences that result in prejudices and distinctions in which one group is exalted above another are always bad and to be opposed, but differences which emphasize only differences on the same plane are to be desired. They are to be sought out, it seems to me, cultivated, and understood.

More than religious differences are involved in maintaining cultural differences. America is fast reaching a point where regional distinctions of custom, speech, idiom are disappearing. All Americans can now listen to the same radio entertainers, watch the same television performers, see the same movies. The colorful metaphorist of the Southern hill country is becoming simply a television creation; Bob Burns and Will Rogers, who had some claim to authenticity in their regionalism, are being replaced by the more artificial, more specifically "entertaining" Tennessee Ernie Ford, who has only the vaguest, non-geographical claim to speaking the idiom of a "back home" that is never located. (Herb Shriner is an exception, although the specific Hoosier content of his material is getting less and less.) Indeed, a regionalist comedian may find himself sharing the bill on such a homogenizing show as Ed Sullivan's with an intellectual, New York type, like Sam Levenson or Shelley Berman, with Sullivan or one of the comedians themselves urging on us the "universality" of all this.

Sam Levenson's career is a striking illustration of the current need to wipe out all differences. Although he has never denied his Jewishness or his origin (Brooklyn), or changed his name, and his jokes are always specifically about Mama and his large family of brothers and sisters and a typically patriarchal Jewish father, he keeps insisting that his experiences have been shared in the small towns of Oklahoma and the Midwest, and in the large cities of the West Coast and Canada, *by everyone*. To a degree, this is no doubt true; every boy who grew up in the twenties probably remembers the water pan under the icebox which had to be emptied regularly, the new crystal set, the Victrola that had to be wound by hand or Caruso would suddenly start sounding like a dying cat. But the point of his humor, the slant from which things are viewed, the values of Mama (who cleaned the house before a maid came: "I should let a stranger see my dirty house?") or of Papa (who would line up the brood and roundly smack each one every so often: "If I don't know why I hit you, then you do.")—all these are quintessentially Jewish. They may have universal overtones, analogues with other cultural situations, but their idiom, their essence, is Jewish. And it is this particularized character that should be preserved, whether it is Jewish, Irish, Negro, Texan, Okie, hill-billy, Indian, or anything else.

With the most skillfully embodied intentions, it is often impossible to fool the audience at large for very long. Gertrude Berg for years with great success played Molly Goldberg on radio and for a shorter period on television. So long as she remained in the Bronx, and so long as she authentically represented a familiar image of a Bronx Jewish housewife, she was accepted. When she moved to the suburb, and tried to convince television watchers that she was a fashionable young suburban matron, with no specific group identity, audiences failed to buy the portrait.

There is danger, no doubt, in keeping up a too keen awareness of cultural differences of any sort, whether they be ethnic, religious, racial, regional, or even personal. No question that prejudice, discrimination, segregation are vicious. They are based on false premises: that Texans are superior, Negroes inferior, Jews richer, Scotsmen thriftier. Whatever particle of truth there may be in any of these propositions grows into a mountain of untruth. And even when the description is absolutely true, the fact can so easily be distorted into something evil and sinister and viciously untrue: God would not have made Negroes black if He did not want us to keep them down. But this is a risk which, I think, must be taken, for cultural pluralism is worth maintaining at any risk.

Moreover, cultural monism, the leveling and blurring of all distinctions, creates its own pernicious, antidemocratic tendencies. Consider the question of the Indians of the Southwest. One school believes that the Indians should not be kept "apart" on reservations, occasionally likened to "concentration camps" (a totally misleading, even vicious comparison), but should be allowed simply to blend with the larger population around them. This group believes the Indian should be helped to abandon his ancient way of life and become fully "American," with no distinctions, legal or cultural or social or educational, between him and "other" Americans. Experts who know the situation agree that such a "dispersal" into the American way of life of Indians would be disastrous. Indians are simply still too "different" from other Americans. Few graduate from college, for example, simply because they cannot adjust to the competitive individualism of American education; the notion of being *individually* tested and evaluated is still alien to many. Language problems, principally of concept and idiom, are enormous.

Yet, obviously, we cannot as a society simply keep the Indians as objects in a kind of "living museum." Disease, illiteracy, superstition, ignorance, poverty must be alleviated, wiped out. But why can't improvements be made without destroying the Indians' identity, uprooting him from his homeland, dispersing him throughout American cities? And, of course, the present tendency is to do just this, to allow the Indian to move his own way toward separateness or assimilation, maintaining his identity and differentness in the process.

In the thirties, some of the extreme leftist sects insisted that the ideal in civilization was to ignore all differences, to ignore the different skins of Asiatics and Africans, to ignore different languages, to ignore various cultural habits, and, above all, to ignore religious differences. Negroes did not have black skins, it was insisted, and I seem to recall particular satisfaction in the leftist press when a Negro actor appeared in *white face* for a Broadway play. This insistence on wiping out all references or consciousness of obvious distinctions was not only a matter of confusion in thought but in party line. In the Soviet Union itself, held up as the great model where racial "discrimination" by law cannot exist, much attention has always been paid to small national groups, to the preservation of local custom and costume (excluding always the religious aspects, of course), and to teaching other languages and dialects than the national one.

The confusion in thought still prevails. It is concluded that because a question is asked about race, religion, color, or other group affiliations, consequently some "discrimination" is about to be exercised, the refusal of a job, the refusal of entry to college or medical school or a social club. But distinctions (as opposed to "discriminations") must be made all the time or we find ourselves led into weirdly blind alleys. I remember a newly appointed dean wanting to find out something about the background of his students at one of New York's city colleges. He prepared an elaborate questionnaire for them to answer, including questions on how many papers the family read, what kind of work the father did, where the parents were born, where the family spent their vacations, what subjects were discussed at the dinner table, and so on, but *not one question about religion, or the like*. Yet the student body was over eighty per cent Jewish, a fact that would have probably revealed more about the students than the entire lengthy form. When I asked the dean why this question was excluded, he answered huffily that "in a democratic college" one couldn't be interested in differences of religion.

During World War II, in the air-crew testing program, it was found that a Jewish boy would probably make an excellent navigator, a good bombardier, a poor pilot. (Of course, there were many individual exceptions; this finding was merely "statistical," applying to thousands and thousands of cases.) Yet the testing authorities felt they could never ask a cadet bluntly whether he was Jewish, however meaningful the question might be in selection. They did get their answer by asking a series of questions based on well-established sociological facts about most American Jews: how large a city did you come from; were your parents born in this country; what business is your family in, etc.

A similar reluctance to identify the group characteristics of tested cadets led to one collection of data having to be discarded. Negro aviation cadets at Tuskegee were selected as a control group although not identified as Negroes. Their scores were significantly higher on certain parts of the test than those of apparently equal similar groups. It was quickly realized, as soon as their Negro identity was established, that they constituted a far above average group since, under the segregated training then in force, only superior Negro young men could become cadets.

A simple and "nondiscriminating" recognition of Jewish or Negro cadets would have avoided much waste in either case, without harming any group or individual. Such a recognition existed with regard to certain American Indian tribes, whose languages, it was felt, would be incomprehensible to Germans or Japanese. Many American Indian soldiers communicated field messages where code was impossible.

Most newspapers throughout the country have been prevailed on to eliminate from their columns the identification of an individual as "Negro." While such identification has often been irrelevant, and sometimes malicious, it is surely essential to understanding certain events to know that some of the individuals involved in a news event are "Negro," or "Jewish," or even Texan. The blanket exclusion of identifying labels has probably led to more harm being done than good. While Julius and Ethel Rosenberg, for example, were undoubtedly understood widely to be Jewish, because of their names, it was not equally widely understood that Fuchs, their British counterpart, whose last name is not uncommon among Jews, was *not* Jewish. I think it a matter of some newsworthiness, too, to know that the distinguished attorneys before the Supreme Court who represented the South's case against integration were opposed by equals who were Negro.

Private colleges that try to recruit a student body that is broadly representative of the country's population and cultural and economic levels as a whole, a representation generally considered useful in itself in education, have an especially difficult time operating under the restriction which forbids them from asking questions about identity. Even religious institutions, or organizations sponsored by religious groups, may not ask questions of prospective employees about religious identity or preference. Farcical situations can result. A Jewish social organization once tried to hire a non-Jewish telephone operator to monitor the switchboard on Jewish holidays. All sorts of repercussions developed.

It is easy enough to understand the motive behind ordinances forbidding the raising of questions as to group: for many years a nasty policy prevailed in many organizations of not hiring Jews, Negroes, Catholics, Italians, and members of other minority groups. These anti-discrimination laws may have improved the situation to a degree for many of these minorities although any determined employer, as the multitude of infractions of the laws testifies, could find a way to circumvent them. What they also did is aid in establishing what I consider the pernicious notion that differences do not exist in our society, or at least should not be recognized. And what does not exist or is not recognized can never be appreciated.

My position is an ambiguous one. While I believe in pluralism, I also believe in assimilation. But I believe in an assimilation in which differences are maintained, not erased. I do not believe that differences should be grouped in isolation from each other. I do not believe in the "separate but equal" notion. I find uncomfortable the resorts of the Catskills or of Florida which are patronized only by Jews, many of whom have changed their family names from the traditional Jewish ones to noncommittal "American" ones, and who insist on following traditional American vacation pastimes "with their own sort." They thus have indeed achieved a type of identification with the American way, but it is exactly the same type which for so many years they were themselves excluded from. The occasional non-Jewish visitor to such Jewish establishments is as much a curiosity as the occasional Jewish one used to be to the country clubs of the twenties, in the novels of Fitzgerald or of Sinclair Lewis. These Jews have "assimilated" much more coarsely and perhaps more dishonestly than any light-colored Negro who has left his community to "pass" among whites. In part, this may still be a dietary problem: many Jews still feel they must follow dietary laws on vacation. But to a much larger extent, to judge from the advertisements in the travel pages of the Sunday *New York Times*, it is a matter of assimilation by exclusion—"we'll be like everyone else by ourselves." Most of the resorts advertise that they serve both Jewish delicacies and "French cooked" lobster and shrimp dishes, foods that are taboo under the laws of kashruth.

It is, of course, in the larger cities and in mass production industries that differences are both maintained and disregarded. It seems to me far less healthy to know that someone is Jewish, Catholic, Italian, Texan, Oklahoman, and always to have to pretend not to know this, than to acknowledge with the crude bluntness made popular in war movies that someone is a "Yid," or a "Spick," or a

"Dago," and then proceed quite plainly with the business at hand in terms of the individual involved. Many places in the country today make no discrimination in membership of country clubs, or other local social organizations. While the conventional American ribbing at such establishments may not be quite so raw and honest as in war films, it does take place with a healthy degree of openness.

I suppose it is on university campuses, in advertising offices, in medical installations, in Hollywood, that it is possible to accommodate most comfortably and yet retain one's identity as a member of some special group in America. Among professional or talented groups, it is skill or productivity that matters.

Some two decades after Hitler we are moving into a new era regarding differences among the multitude of groups in America. The danger is not so much that we will continue to insist on making invidious distinctions, comparing one group unfavorably with another, as that in an exuberance of good will, we'll start insisting that there are no differences at all, that we must close our eyes to differences, that differences are "bad."

Differences are good. Differences of opinion, class, taste, judgment, habit, costume, value, politics, race, religion, general beliefs—these differences are precisely what distinguish the United States from countries with more homogeneous backgrounds. Differences, it has been said over and over again, stimulate vitality; they introduce new ideas, new possibilities, new strategies of approach and response to everything: industry, scholarship, science, medicine, sports, architecture, dress-designing.

Some have argued that what is wrong with America is that it has too heterogeneous a background, that it is "hybrid," that it hasn't a single strand of tradition reaching back indefinitely. But this is exactly what is right with our country. Our tradition is one of differences among union. It may have become corny after a while for all of the Hollywood war films to keep emphasizing the melting-pot character of every infantry cadre, but, in a sense, this was one of the points the country was making in fighting the war, that we are a nation of different individuals, different *and* individual, and that we wanted to maintain it that way.

I am not calling merely for a recognition of differences; I am calling for a celebration of differences, a determined consciousness of differences. We have reached a point of maturity in our development as a nation where we can at least begin to acknowledge our motley character. It will be a while yet, perhaps, before we can fully appreciate or enjoy it, but a beginning must be made. *Vive les différences!*

FIFTEEN

THE NONCONFORMIST ATTACK ON RELIGION

NONCONFORMISTS spend much time attacking religion. Whatever else they may disagree upon, they agree in deriding religion in one aspect or another, whether they sneer at Billy Graham, Norman Vincent Peale, or Bishop Fulton J. Sheen, whether they echo the Marxist clichés about churches being the opiate of the people, whether they scoff at the "religious revival" in recent years, or whether they challenge, very simply and fundamentally, the existence of God. I heard a university intellectual declare bluntly and bitterly that anyone who believed in God was "plain stupid." On a higher plane, a contributor to a *Partisan Review* symposium, "Religion and the Intellectuals," dismissed "the recurrent interest in religion today" as "a sign that the great effort of emancipation that began three centuries ago has not been successful, or at least has not completed its work."

What I find astonishing in the nonconformist glib dismissal of religion and God is its phenomenal naïveté; I suppose this dates back to the easy atheism of the radical thirties. A mature and "highbrow" college professor I know actually believes that he settled the whole issue of God at the time he threw open his office window, stuck his head out, and challenged God to prove His existence by striking him dead then and there. (This is a typical enough ritual on college campuses. One boy got a clod of mud thrown into his face when he went through this procedure.) Equally unsophisticated is the challenge posed by nonconforming atheists to describe God, to locate His abode, to offer "scientific" proof of His nature, and so on.

The attack on organized religion, leaving aside the question of God for the moment, is somewhat more sophisticated. It is based ultimately, however, on the exposé notion of history. Once you find out the details about the formation and growth of any church, you explain away its ideals and principles. Many of the Popes were corrupt; the Crusades were mainly commercial enterprises; the rise of Calvinism paralleled the rise of the middle class. This is much like the easy cynicism about our national ideals that developed at the time the economic interpretation of the Constitution became popular.

But one doesn't have to go to history for this sort of attack. You can cite the "religious" articles in any issue of the *Reader's Digest*, the spiritually "uplifting" books by Liebman or Peale. The unction, the shabbiness of the content, its superficiality and glibness, are all supposed to prove on the face of it the bankruptcy of modern religion, the foolishness of belief. And, of course, the Catholic Church always comes in for particularly strong and sustained attack.

Now, of course, many of the complaints have a good deal of truth in them. I am not suggesting that our magazine and television religious oracles are pillars of intellectual wisdom. But the attacks on them would have been made whatever they were. Niebuhr, Tillich, Kierkegaard, Buber, Barth—intellectuals all, whatever momentary fashionableness any of them may enjoy—are as much subject to the same offhand dismissal as their mass-production counterparts. I have often heard these men dismissed in the corridors and classrooms of Columbia University and in the offices of intellectual magazines. Sidney Hook, a leading professional intellectual, will not allow that theological inquiry might have an intellectual content. "What these God-seeking intellectuals are looking for," he wrote in the *Partisan Review* discussion, "is not so much a theology but a theodicy, not merely, or even primarily, truth but justification and comfort." And not often is it felt necessary to document factually and rationally attacks on the Catholic Church.

I am not talking of the serious and sober critique of religion that has long been carried on by such thinkers as Will Herberg and by Sidney Hook himself. Nor do I have in mind attempts to understand, to describe in hard, uncompromising detail, the insides and outsides of modern religious institutions. The kind of snide and picayune attacks I have in mind have no intention of understanding the character of religion. They are simply thoughtless gestures dictated by fashion, or triggered by an adolescent notion of emancipation.

The results are pernicious. It is positively disreputable in many intellectual and all nonconformist circles to bring up seriously the question of God (as risky to one's status as it once was to mention Trotsky in a group of Stalinists). A discussion of Kierkegaard must be assumed to begin from a premise of settled atheism. An "enlightened" student in a graduate seminar on Milton kept smirking to himself during a discussion of the doctrinal basis of *Para-*

dise Lost. "The poem is funny," he said. "Milton actually believed in God." It becomes difficult to criticize meaningfully the vulgarities of Hollywood Biblical spectaculars. Since you are not supposed to take either Hollywood or the Bible seriously, what is the point of carping? It even becomes impossible to hold to a serious atheism: disbelief becomes a casual, obvious, taken-for-granted matter, not worth the trouble of critical examination and reexamination.

Here as elsewhere, nonconformism is marked by an intolerance matched only by old-fashioned religious intolerance itself. The nonconformist makes no attempt to understand, much less to analyze, the nature of contemporary religious interest and expression. Ritualistic himself, he denies anyone else the solace of any ritual but his own. Narrow of vision, he cannot see worthy areas outside his own focus. He attributes simple-mindedness, charlatanism, obscurantism to anyone committed positively to religion, even to anyone still skeptically uncommitted. At his kindliest, he "psychologizes" or "historicizes" belief, explaining it away, "accounting" for it, "excusing" and "forgiving" the poor, misguided, confused believer.

It is the rise of nonconformism in recent years, I would suggest, which has been responsible for the notion that America is going through a "religious revival." Actually, as Professor S. Martin Lipset, University of California sociologist, pointed out, there is no religious revival. Religious affiliation and observance today is only about as widespread as it has ever been in this country. Nonconformists, I contend, have simply directed a new attention to it. Religion and God are especially big targets for small minds pretending to superiority. (They are, of course, big targets for genuinely big and superior minds, but such minds respect the elusiveness and worthiness of the target.)

What nonconformists have made it difficult to do is examine the facts of the situation as they actually are. They have also made it difficult, as I have said, to conduct a serious dialogue on the nature of God in the modern world. Intellect today in America, to retain its respectability, must never turn its attention on all sorts of taboo areas, religion being perhaps the most prominent. If it does happen to consider questions of religion, there are ready formulas, ready attitudes, for the examination. Let an intellectual depart from the formulas, abandon the attitudes, and he risks the charge of being trivial or foolish.

Yet the sociological meanings of America's religious institutions are profound and widespread in their implications. As Professor Lipset has written, "The 'fecundity' of American Protestantism in producing new sects seems to result from the marriage in this society of the democratic value of free expression of all political ideas with the Protestant stress on the obligation to follow individual conscience. The norms of political tolerance and religious tolerance, expressed in democratic and religious institutions, have reinforced each other." Professor Lipset, of course, has pioneered in probing the true character of American religious practice and its implications in politics. His findings have been enlightening and valuable, but he has had to cut through the nonconformist curtain which offered its own offhand, sketchy, one-dimensional image.

Nor are the theological aspects of the subject any less significant. So determined has the onslaught of organized nonconformism been against belief that I have heard two clergymen, one of whom was actually a professor at a seminary, express cynical disbelief in God. When I challenged him about the inconsistency of continuing in his profession and rejecting the existence of God, he shrugged. "I see no reason why an atheist cannot be a clergyman," he said. Both of these men, and many others I am sure, find it easier to accommodate to the current dogmas of intellectual nonconformism than to hold to their faiths. But this is the critical question, isn't it? Isn't the problem of God in the modern world exactly the rock on which belief today should break itself, or on which it should build? The French thinkers have seen this clearly, whatever their conclusions; they have not glibly dismissed the issue with a smirk. In America, in the circles of intellectual nonconformism, at any rate, we handle the problem, or pretend that we do, by talking of hidden persuasion or status-seeking, or by deriding Peale and Graham and Herman Wouk, or by attacking Catholic positions on abortion and birth control. We mow down straw men and pretend they are giants.

It seems clear to me that if we are not to allow the questions of belief and of God to be relegated to the nonconformist dump of dismissed issues it will be necessary to break out of the nonconformist patterns of the dialogue. If we are to find values more significant than those of passing fashion or empty ritual, we must consider religion and God seriously, independently, originally. We must not fear to come to unpopular conclusions, whether of commitment or rejection, or even of simple skepticism.

SIXTEEN

HOW FREE IS FREE?

THE FUNDAMENTAL issue in the question of conformity is freedom. The nonconformist insists that only he is truly free. Only he resists the mass pressures of our contemporary society. Only he exercises individualism and independence. But, as I have tried to argue, it is in conformity that one finds the richest possibilities for varied, for authentic, for meaningful freedom. The freedom of nonconformity is an empty and idle freedom.

My case is most obvious and easiest to prove, I suppose, against fashionable, conforming nonconformity. The exclusions, the taboos, the enthusiasms, the stereotyped evaluations, the automatic responses—these are as formalized for the professional nonconformist as the text and movement of any church ritual. You can almost exactly predict the behavior, the reactions, the very words and gestures of this ritualist under all sorts of conditions and stimuli. Coffee houses, east coast and west coast and in between, are crawling with identical types. It is not that there is some kind of central organization, a nonconformist union, laying down rules of speech and behavior, details of costume. It's simply that the patterns of nonconformism are ready at hand for anyone to adopt once you accept the basic premise that anything popular or conventional or supported by a majority or catering to the people is in and of itself bad: advertising, popular songs, movies, automobiles, ties, ranch houses. The mechanical nonconformists betray their cause in the very process of advocating it: as I have said, they are eager to ram their values down everyone's throat. Nor is it necessary to adopt the code of the nonconformist in every detail to practice occasional and partial nonconformism with as much smug satisfaction as the fanatic.

But I think I can make my point even if I exclude the mindless robots. Nonconformism, if it remains true to itself, must ultimately become free-floating, asocial, abstract, unrelated to a context. The absolute nonconformist, of course, would be the man on a desert island. This is extreme, obviously, but we often see close approximations to this ideal.

The desert-island nonconformist differs from the fashionable one as much as he does from the conformist himself. The desert-island man lives without a society around him. He knows little of the news, nothing about popular things; he cannot carry on social conversations; he is unaware of his dress; he does not vote or listen to the radio or watch television; in short, he carries around him total insulation from the daily world. He lives at the heart of an egocentric circle. If he is an expert in a particular field, he is likely to be ignorant of contiguous or parallel fields, let alone unrelated ones.

What kind of freedom is this? Robinson Crusoe on his island had this freedom. Anyone isolated from the rest of mankind—the lighthouse keeper, the weather-station man in the Arctic, the savage in the jungle—has this freedom. If we live in any society, we live, as Rousseau defined the matter, by a social contract. We live with a consciousness of the presence and needs of other persons.

The desert-island nonconformist may have the excuse for his isolation that he is not willful; he is simply unaware. His behavior, his alienation, is not a matter of ideology but of personality. It is instinctive, not chosen. Whatever his excuse or explanation, the fact remains that he is at the extreme end of nonconformism. He is indeed an ideal for many conscious conformists. While in society, he is simultaneously outside it. He has his cake while he eats it.

But is not such a type as trapped by his limitations as Crusoe was? Are not all sorts of experiences and possibilities closed to him? Consider the nonconformists who boast of not ever watching television or going to the movies or nightclubs or paying attention to advertisements. Nonconformism in such instances is not the free exercise of taste. It is not connected with the reasoned rejection of a particular object. It rejects everything in a class. This is not discrimination any more than the Russian rejection of anything capitalistic is a matter of choice. This is behavior of the most restricted, most imprisoned sort. Our professional nonconformists are as much prisoners of their reflexes as Pavlov's dogs.

It is certainly nothing new to say that freedom can only exist within society. Society after all is responsible for creature comforts. Only society offers any real possibilities for minimizing poverty, for easing ill health. Poor and diseased, how free can we be? But society offers everything else in addition to basic comforts. Our freedom means something only insofar as we can think, talk, act, move about freely (within the usual limits that our freedom does not infringe on anyone else's). We can think only in the contexts of history, of knowledge, of acquaintance with writings and works of art. We can feel only in relation to ourselves and other persons. These are social things. It would mean nothing to say we could talk or move about freely if there were not the means to do either widely: freedom of speech in a public park or at the American exposition in Moscow (reported by some of the American aides of outspoken Russian visitors criticizing their government) do not compare with such freedom in the press or on radio or television, all social media; the right to move about means little without the socially created devices of the train, the plane, the automobile. What does it mean to feel freely if we cannot express or suggest our feelings in some social way?

The great complaint nonconformists make about society, of course, is that it restricts thought, speech, behavior; that it imposes values, judgments, tastes. Conformism to them is opposed to individualism, to uniqueness. But it must be clear to anyone of independent mind that conformism in the western world in the mid-twentieth century encourages and rewards handsomely all sorts of cranky, crotchety, highly individualistic responses. Some of the most popular books on the best-seller lists week after week are tracts against our times, against cars, against advertising, against movies, against schools, against big companies, against politics. Indeed many of these conform so totally to a pattern of tone that they are anything but unique. These books are often nothing but a violation of the quite genuine freedom within our "conformist" society: they pretend to be daring and bold and iconoclastic; they are often nothing more than sophomoric, repetitive, and flatulent. If I were looking for evidence to *prove* that our society was actually a conforming one, I would cite just these shallow pretensions to independently critical thought.

No doubt the situation is confused by paradoxes. A thinker like Hayek, whose philosophy is poised on the one great point of "freedom," is considered conservative, "illiberal," even reactionary. The "nonconformist" pundits advocate all sorts of government involvement in our affairs (and often not unjustly, I hasten to add, lest someone jump to the conclusion that I am an adherent of Hayek's position).

Over and over again we can cite from our personal experiences examples of conservatives and "conformists" who are far more tolerant, independent, original than the persons we know who insist on flaunting their identity as "liberals" and "nonconformists." An acquaintance of mine who parrots current nonconformist slogans as earnestly as any church dogma once described himself to me as "one hundred and ten per cent nonconformist." (At that he may have been right: exceeding one hundred per cent, he may have been turning back on himself.) Nonconformists are prone to label by stereotypes, to see the world and all its issues and all its peoples in monochromatic black or white.

As one looks at the current social scene without blinders or distorting lenses, I think he will clearly see that our so-called conformists, our Babbitts and "conservatives," grant more freedom to dissenters than our self-styled nonconformists—beatniks, bohemians, and bums though they may be. Nonconformists are so insistent on easy, glib, all-inclusive labels because they are, after all, lonely and lost. They are air people, floating away from society in balloons; they want company on their lonely, vagrant journeys. And since they, like all persons, need a sense of society, they create a kind of anti-society, in which all the usual values of society are sternly turned topsy-turvy. Their freedom is like the freedom of persons under Communism; their love is the love of *1984;* their final nonconformity is a thoroughly disciplined conformity.

Freedom cannot exist in a vacuum. Freedom has meaning only in a context: free where? free when? free to do what? free from whom? In Shaw's play *Saint Joan,* Joan rejects the "freedom" to remain alive if she has to remain so for the rest of her days in prison. Shaw knew what freedom meant under all circumstances; it was never simply a gesture unrelated to a time and a place. Was not Socrates the object of attack of the "enlightened thinkers" of his society?

Conformists recognize that freedom is rooted not only in a society but in an individual. We can be free only to the degree that this means something in society and to the degree that it means something to us personally. How free is the person driven by unconscious forces? It is the nonconformist who is arrogant about his independence. He rejects the notion that he may be his own worst censor, his own worst tyrant. All of Freudian theory is rooted in a full, deep, circumstantial sense of society, past and present, in all of its dimensions. Freud was entirely a man of his milieu. Freudians recognize well that conformism need not be an escape or an evasion of true individuality, but may be an aid to it. We must recognize reality, know where we are, before we can leave it. The nonconformists in their bursts and fits of alienation are always making fairy-tale journeys. They are terrified by bogeymen and mirages. Only the conformists can make real departures, can arrive anywhere.

The conformism I talk about, it must be clear, is not the empty minded, follow-the-leader kind of thing nonconformists are always so gleefully and cheaply attacking. But even follow-the-leader conformism is less invidious than doctrinaire nonconformism, because it makes no pretense of being anything but conformism; it simply does not know any better.

The conformism I have in mind, the sort in which real liberty is rooted, is merely based on a recognition of reality, on an acceptance of the limitations of existence (both social and individual), and on an indifference to affectations and poses advertising some phony uniqueness. One mark of the genuinely free man is that he will not casually make a value judgment as to the comparative merit in and of themselves of an abstract conformism or nonconformism *out of context*. The truly free man does not find it necessary to prove his freedom either by asserting it blatantly for himself or denying its presence contemptuously in others. He is free to make the multitudes of decisions and responses it is necessary to make to live with the greatest self-realization and self-expression in our world; he is not bound by any party to predetermined stands. He can like or not like a particular wine. He can choose to buy or not to buy a particular automobile. He can choose to follow or ignore fashion—in furniture, clothes, politics, movies, music, writing, foods, homes. He can choose to vote or not to vote for the current great liberal. He can afford to exercise this kind of gross independence because he knows that only so can he be free, free of the petty nose-thumbing of rejection, free of the thoughtless embraces of acceptance.

Perhaps what we need, here as in so many other places,

is a new vocabulary. The barbarous phrase "conforming nonconformist" is accurate enough, but it is clearly paradoxical. All I am criticizing, I hope it is clear, is conformism, blind acceptance of any dogma, however it masks itself, however much it pretends to be nonconformism. I do believe that in the present scene nonconformism has betrayed itself shabbily. It has been guilty of far more dishonesty and distortion and deception than the most narrow conformism has ever been. Nonconformism for intellectuals—for persons of any sophistication and character—seems to me bankrupt.

I speak well of conformists, and I identify myself as one (to my astonishment), because I find in it much healtheir possibilities than in contemporary nonconformism. Precisely because I do believe that "individuality" and "independence" are to be cherished, I argue against a nonconformist cant which insists on defining "individuality" and "independence" by mob logic and mob technique. I assert that creativity and originality never follow patterns; I believe that they must be related to a responsive and responsible sense of the total world; I suggest that they may come most meaningfully in our time from that sort of conformism which works within the more limited bounds of necessity and possibility rather than those extravagantly unlimited ones of an arrogant willfulness.

Whenever I confess to conformism defiantly, I feel silly. One should not really take seriously the ominous strictures, the finger-pointing postures, of our nonconformist oracles. These prophetic discussions of our times are often about as profound as an exchange at the office water-cooler. In this respect, I suppose I am, without qualification or apology, a genuine enough conformist. The world's issues are more important than the problems that bother us daily, the ones concerned with chrome or coffee or calypso. There are the classical concerns of history and art, life and study, scholarship and science, philosophy and love. I am happy to confess that I am the sort of conformist who finds himself in the end bored by diatribes, frivolous or earnest, against fleeting phenomena. Even fashionable nonconformism, oppressive as it is, may, in the large perspective, be only a temporary aberration. At least, I hope we can make it so.